∞

*Six Lessons for Life
from the
School of the Cross*

Other books
from Sophia Institute Press®
by John A. Kane:

*Conquering Your Sins
With Heartfelt Repentance*

The School of Mary
*Forty Essential Lessons for Sinners,
from the Blessed Mother Herself*

*Transforming Your Life
Through the Eucharist*

John A. Kane

Six Lessons for Life
from the
School of the Cross

How the Cross Can Bring You
Peace of Mind, Joy of Heart,
and Strength of Soul

SOPHIA INSTITUTE PRESS®
Manchester, New Hampshire 03108

Six Lessons for Life from the School of the Cross was originally published in 1947 by The Declan X. McMullen Company, New York, under the title *The School of the Cross*. This 1999 edition by Sophia Institute Press contains minor editorial revisions to the original text.

Sophia Institute Press®
Box 5284, Manchester, NH 03108
1-800-888-9344
www.sophiainstitute.com

Nihil obstat: John M. A. Fearns, S.T.D., Censor
Imprimatur: Francis Cardinal Spellman, Archbishop of New York
Ascension Thursday, 1947

Library of Congress Cataloging-in-Publication Data

Kane, John A. 1883-
    [School of the cross]
    Six lessons for life from the school of the cross : how the cross can bring you peace of mind, joy of heart, and strength of soul / John A. Kane.
       p. cm.
    Originally published: The school of the cross. New York : D.X. McMullen, 1947.
    Includes bibliographical references.
    ISBN 0-918477-97-2 (pbk. : alk. paper)
    1. Jesus Christ — Passion Meditations. I. Title.
BT453.K33   1999
248.8′6 — dc21   99-30543 CIP

99 00 01 02 03 10 9 8 7 6 5 4 3 2 1

To the memory of
Reverend
Daniel I. McDermott

Contents

∞

Introduction

Editor's note: The biblical references in the following pages are based on the Douay-Rheims edition of the Old and New Testaments. Where applicable, biblical quotations have been cross-referenced with the differing names and numeration in the Revised Standard Version, using the following symbol: (RSV =).

∞

Introduction

∞

Consciously or unconsciously, willingly or unwillingly, all of us are pupils in the school of the Cross. Our first step in true wisdom will be our recognition of this fact. Our next step will be a resolution to pursue our course of study in a docile mood.

It is not amiss to add that the three statements above are not ascetical assumptions or theories, but simple facts. First of all, we are inescapably pupils in the worldwide school. "Dost thou think to escape that which no mortal ever could avoid?" It is the golden book of the *Imitation* that propounds this query. And from that early dawn of human events when God cursed the earth, down to the last syllable of recorded time, the experience of our fallen race has been repeating, and will continue endlessly reiterating, the answer of the monk of Kempen: "Dispose and order all things as thou wilt, and as seems best to thee; and thou wilt still find something to suffer, either willingly or unwillingly, and so thou shalt find the Cross."[1]

The sweat of Adam's brow, in which alone he should eat bread,[2] was but a symbol of all the elements in our litany of

---

[1] St. Thomas à Kempis (c. 1380-1471; ascetical writer), *Imitation of Christ*, Bk. 2, ch. 12.

[2] Cf. Gen. 3:19.

suffering. The synonyms are many: pain, torture, anguish, sorrow, despair; or the lesser troubles of life: disappointments, longings, desires, disturbance of ease, hunger, thirst, laborious days, sleepless nights. The Cross, too, has broadened its symbolism. The word has become a common noun, and we speak, without any necessarily spiritual or Christian implication, of the crosses met within our daily lives.

In the widest sense, then, every human being must, consciously or unconsciously, willingly or unwillingly, live his life in the school of the Cross.

Many have lived in that school without conscious recognition of it. They found, with Ecclesiastes, that all their days were full of sorrows and miseries, their nights without rest for their minds.[3] With alternating hopes and fears, they wandered rather than walked through their allotted time, uncertain of the way or of the journey's end. For them, experience was not the best teacher, for her instructions fell on deaf ears and, in any event, would have been inadequate to meet their real needs.

Many, however, have lived consciously in such a school and have striven to formulate for their brethren the wisest lessons in the philosophy of life.

In general, we associate two things with what is called the Epicurean ideal: first, the unwearied search after whatever pleasures might be found on earth; second, the devising of such arrangements as might be possible to each person in order to avoid disturbance of ease or comfort — in brief, the dream of rest such as that of the lotus-eaters in Homer's epic

---

[3] Cf. Eccles. 2:23.

the *Odyssey*. The philosophy was a failure. Ecclesiastes tells us that he tried the experiment with conscious and capable endeavors, and found only vanity and vexation of spirit.[4] The Roman poet Horace believed in the theory, but nevertheless has left an imperishable legacy to mankind in his "Ode to Grosphus." Seek after pleasure as we may, we cannot escape Grim Care:

> Grim Care the nightly train attends,
> Grim Care the beaked ship ascends,
> Outstrips the Stag, and the east wind
> That chases clouds, leaves far behind.[5]

On the other hand, the Stoics counseled patient fortitude. Their ideal has been partially summed up in the familiar counsel: "What can't be cured must be endured." Perhaps they shared the thought expressed by James Clarence Mangan in *The Wail and Warning of the Three Khalen Deers*, that "Life's a sad experiment." They determined to make the best of a bad bargain, as it were, to cultivate natural virtue and to take everything with philosophic calm.

This "calm" approaches the Epicurean idea of "rest." Peace, quiet, rest — we need that something, and long for it. We echo the old cry of the psalmist: "Who will give me wings like a dove, and I will fly and be at rest?"[6]

The Christian, too, should have his conscious philosophy of life. He is human and is therefore inevitably subject to "the

---

[4] Cf. Eccles. 1:14.
[5] *Odes*, Bk. 3, no. 1.
[6] Ps. 54:7 (RSV = Ps. 55:6).

slings and arrows of outrageous fortune."[7] His alone is the true school of the Cross.

Those who have studied best in that school have constructed an amazing philosophy. Its lessons have been inculcated partly by personal experience, partly by that Christian history which is for them nothing less than philosophy teaching by examples. St. Augustine, like Ecclesiastes, spoke the bittersweet lesson of experience when he cried out: "Our hearts, O God, Thou hast made for Thyself, and they cannot rest until they rest in Thee!"[8] We can hope to find rest only in that school of the Cross, whose divine Founder and abiding Teacher has invited us all to enter it. If we come to Him with our labors and burdens, He will refresh us, but only on condition that we take His yoke upon us and learn of Him certain lessons that affright our human nature — meekness and humility, for instance, and the art of following Him by bearing our own cross.

Yet this philosophy is amazing, not only in its invitation to suffering, but in the results attained by docile obedience as well. Take His yoke upon you, "and you shall find rest to your souls."[9] Stranger still is the assurance that His "yoke is sweet," His "burden light."[10]

Yet, it is true. For those who have conformed their lives to this amazing philosophy have tasted and seen how sweet is the

---

[7] William Shakespeare, *Hamlet,* Act 3, scene 1.

[8] St. Augustine (354-430; Bishop of Hippo), *Confessions*, Bk. 1, ch. 1.

[9] Matt. 11:29.

[10] Matt. 11:30.

Lord.[11] In some mysterious fashion, they have been able to transmute pain into joy.

Thus St. Paul could write: "I exceedingly abound with joy in all our tribulation."[12] Only through a mist of superabounding joy could St. Francis Xavier[13] see the pages in which he was setting down, for his superiors afar off, the story of his overwhelming sufferings. St. Teresa[14] could exclaim: "Either suffering or death!" St. Mary Magdalen de Pazzi[15] could amend this into: "Suffering rather than death!"

What is the secret of it all? If we have not divined it from the grandest of its expositions — the eagerness of Christ's desire to die for us — it is because we are unwilling pupils in the school of the Cross. But in whatever measure we have appropriated its lessons to our own lives, in that measure we have begun to learn the truest wisdom.

Father Kane's volume will be our guide through the school of the Cross. With a literary grace that presents no initial obstacles to a finely sensitive temperament, the story of the Cross is told briefly and adequately. The phases of the Passion are made to convey their respective moral lessons almost by implication, and what comment is given is stimulating and consoling. We learn that the pathway to true peace is the royal Way of the Cross, and we face with less of our natural repugnance the question of Thomas à Kempis: "Why art thou afraid

[11] Cf. Ps. 33:9 (RSV = Ps. 34:8).
[12] 2 Cor. 7:4.
[13] St. Francis Xavier (1506-1552), Jesuit missionary.
[14] St. Teresa of Avila (1515-1582), Carmelite mystic.
[15] St. Mary Magdalen de Pazzi (1566-1607), Carmelite mystic.

to take up thy cross, which leads to a kingdom? In the Cross is salvation; in the Cross is life; in the Cross is protection from thy enemies. In the Cross is infusion of heavenly sweetness; in the Cross is strength of mind; in the Cross is joy of spirit."[16]

— *Msgr. Hugh T. Henry*

[16] *Imitation of Christ*, Bk. 2, ch. 12.

∞

*Six Lessons for Life
from the
School of the Cross*

Chapter One

Learn to develop true sorrow for sin

∞

The suffering of Christ is the absorbing theme presented to us in the Sacred Scriptures. An undercurrent of immeasurably deep sorrow runs through all the Bible. Throughout the Old and the New Testament, the contemplation of Christ's divinity is secondary to the thought of His abasement. The Savior is ever the "Man of Sorrows."[17] The mind of the sacred writer is so thoroughly preoccupied with Christ's sufferings that there is beneath his words a sorrow ineffable. The suffering of the Redeemer invests the story of His life with a sadness and a sublimity that profoundly stir the deepest sympathy of our hearts.

Christ pressed the chalice of sorrow to His lips at His very birth, for joy unmixed with sorrow, which usually surrounds human births, did not smile upon the divine Child at His nativity. Even in the manger He was "the reproach of men and the outcast of the people," who drove Him to the stable because there was no room for Him in the inn.[18] Deep sorrow was also revealed in the woeful prophecy of Simeon that a sword would pierce the soul of His Virgin Mother[19] — sad

[17] Isa. 53:3.
[18] Ps. 21:7 (RSV = Ps. 22:6); Luke 2:7.
[19] Luke 2:35.

words indeed, which were almost immediately followed by the massacre of the Innocents and by the silently sorrowful flight into Egypt.[20]

For a time, during the beginning of Christ's ministry, the sunshine of joy dispelled the black clouds of sorrow. The first disciples quickly gathered around the Master, attracted by the mysterious magic of His personality. Crowds heard Him, charmed to ecstasy by the words of wisdom which He uttered in the marvelous Sermon on the Mount.[21] The sick and the maimed were brought to Him to be cured. The devils themselves trembled in His presence and were subject to Him. His hold upon the people struck terror into the rulers who feared the loss of their power. The populace was roused to the highest pitch of enthusiasm by a profession of faith expressed by human lips, but inspired by Heaven: "Thou art Christ, the Son of the living God."[22] Such were the signs heralding a triumph beyond all precedent.

∞

Christ constantly anticipated His Passion

But the sunshine of joy was soon to be obscured by the twilight of future trial. The powers of Hell, all this time, were marshaling their forces to arouse in the fickle and wavering multitude intense hatred and relentless opposition. The hypocritical scribes and Pharisees, with their characteristic cunning and duplicity, attribute His miracles to Beelzebub, the prince

---

[20] Matt. 2:13-14, 16.

[21] Matt. 5-7.

[22] Matt. 16:16.

of devils;[23] the disciples, so slow of heart and dull of understanding, begin to forsake and to walk with Him no more;[24] and the soul of the Son of Man is again overshadowed by the sorrow which He foretold at the very beginning of His public ministry. "Destroy this temple," says Christ to the Pharisees, "and in three days I will raise it up."[25] "But He spoke of the temple of His body."[26]

The same cloud of anticipated suffering and death obscures one of the most radiantly bright and beautiful periods of Christ's life, tinging with sadness His words to Nicodemus. "As Moses," says our Lord to this ruler of the Jews, "lifted up the serpent in the desert, so must the Son of Man be lifted up."[27] When St. Peter, with all the intensity of his ardently noble nature, professes his faith in his Master's divinity and exclaims: "Thou art Christ, the Son of the living God," Christ, with prophetic vision, again peers into the future and speaks of that which has stirred the deepest fibers of His soul: His coming death. "But He, strictly charging them, commanded they should tell this to no man, saying: 'The Son of man must suffer many things, and be rejected by the ancients and chief priests and scribes, and be killed.' "[28] The same ominous foreboding dimmed and darkened even the brightness and the glory of His Transfiguration, when "His face did shine as the sun; and

---

[23] Cf. Matt. 12:24.
[24] Cf. John 6:67.
[25] John 2:19.
[26] John 2:21.
[27] John 3:14.
[28] Luke 9:21-22.

His garments became white as snow,"[29] and the chosen three fell prostrate, completely overpowered by the brilliant splendor of His divinity; for Moses and Elijah spoke on Tabor of "His decease that He should accomplish in Jerusalem."[30]

The foresight of suffering intensifies His sorrow. The mind haunted by such a specter is oppressed and collapses before it. We must not forget that Christ's constant anticipation of His Passion made it a terrible reality. This thought is inescapable when we remember that Christ's capacity to suffer was far different from ours.

We are easily distracted and unconsciously turn from one train of thought to another. Even the most poignant sorrows quickly and entirely leave us, because our finite faculties cannot even grasp, much less retain, them with a full realization of their complete meaning. As we are creatures of change, we are readily distracted by change. A shock, a little fatigue, or new surroundings often banish from us the cause of our distress. Moreover, the same idea cannot engage the mind's attention for very long; sometimes a mere trifle will dispel it immediately. Besides, physical ailments tend to weaken the memory and blunt the imagination. Our very frailty and instability thus greatly diminish the bitterness of our sorrow and the pain of suffering. The present evil, engrossing all our powers, soon dulls our vision of future evil.

The oppressiveness of sorrow is measured by the depth and permanence of the sufferer's impressions. The man of coarse nature does not or cannot feel sorrow very keenly, because he

---

[29] Matt. 17:2.
[30] Luke 9:31.

is practically invulnerable to insult. He hardly experiences distress, because his nature is almost fully immune to it.

But Christ's susceptibility to insult and injury and His ability to suffer were great, because His mental faculties were perfect even as man. So perfect was Christ's human intellect that it could be neither disturbed nor distracted. Like the rays of the sun brought to a focus, it was forever fixed on His future Passion and death. He beheld them with a clearness of vision of which our mental powers are incapable, because they are weak and unstable, easily influenced, and distracted by the least variety or change of events. Hence, the words of Holy Scripture: "I walked sorrowful all the day long. . . . My sorrow is continually before me,"[31] are squarely applicable to Him.

The mere reading of the history of the Passion greatly oppresses us. What, then, must have been the constant realization of His future sufferings and death to the God-Man before whose mind they were always vividly present, and who thus experienced them in all the horror of that gruesome detail which defies description!

∞

Christ's Passion has transformed the world

As the Passion is the theme of the Scriptures which colors all of God's dealings with man, so are its effects everywhere visible in this sin-laden world. The death of Christ is the most important fact in history. It has revolutionized society. It has profoundly influenced every phase of human life. It has been the source and support of the highest ideals that can guide

[31] Ps. 37:7, 18 (RSV = Ps. 38:6, 17).

human conduct. It has lifted man from the lowest level of the most sordid selfishness into the higher and nobler regions of spirituality. It is the legion that has conquered naturalism. It is the power that has subdued disordered passions. "Unless the grain of wheat falling into the ground die, itself remaineth alone. But if it die, it bringeth forth much fruit."[32]

Christ's death has produced fruit a hundredfold. A new order of thought has been born of it. It has been the energizing power of a more sublime standard of action, the very heart of a morality which emphasizes the most fundamental and, of all truths, the most vitally significant to man: his supernatural destiny. Its effects have been all-embracing in their scope. The vigor of justice, the strength of love, the quality of mercy that "becomes the throned monarch better than his crown,"[33] gentle peace, heroic self-sacrifice — all were born on the Mount of Crucifixion. Christian civilization with all its inestimable blessings flows from Calvary; and the man who will deny the influence of Christ's death, or will not let its consequences crystallize into action in his life, nonetheless experiences many of its priceless benefits. In the numerous favors lavished upon common humanity by the munificent hand of God, he possesses the earthly blessings of the sufferings and death of Christ, which snatched man from the jaws of Hell and folded him again in the strong arms of the eternally loving Creator.

Like the light of Heaven, the Passion is everywhere visible. It is the essence of God's message to man. It is the sublimely fascinating theme of the Sacred Volume. It is the perennial

[32] John 12:24-25.
[33] William Shakespeare, *The Merchant of Venice*, Act 4, scene 1.

force of the world's progress, because it is the tie between Heaven and earth. As Christ and the Father are one, eternally coexisting, having the same divine nature and substance, so the creature is one with Christ and, in Him, one with the Father through Christ's sufferings and death. The God-Man satisfied the Father for sin not merely by His Incarnation, but by the terrible giving of Himself as a sacrificial victim.

Furthermore, the Passion is the best school in which we may learn to imitate Christ. The virtues and holiness of the Savior are never so powerful in their appeal to the finest sensibilities of the human mind and heart as when seen in the red raiment of His sufferings. Again, our share in His sufferings is the essential condition of our eternal union with Him, for "through many tribulations we must enter into the kingdom of God."[34] "If we suffer, we shall also reign with Him."[35]

∞

Sympathy with Christ springs from sorrow for sin

To meditate profitably upon the Passion, to know Christ more intimately through this marvelous mystery of infinite mercy, and thus to love Him more ardently and to follow Him more closely, we must sympathize with Him in His anguish and pain.

Now, sympathy is something more than weeping with those who weep. It is a realization of the reason for sorrow and a discernment of its most hidden source. To sympathize with another, we must try to feel the sword of sorrow as he feels it;

[34] Acts 14:21.
[35] 2 Tim. 2:12.

we must strive to endure the twinge of suffering as he endures it; we must endeavor, in some measure, to examine the source of his affliction; we must try to sound the depths of his desolation, the hidden cause of his pain.

Sorrow is the sudden or slow awakening of the feelings caused by the piercing and rending of the finer fibers of the human heart. Its nature and its oppressiveness flow from its cause and from the sensitiveness of the sufferer. To understand Christ's sorrow, therefore, we must examine its origin and His mental attitude toward it.

What made Christ the Man of Sorrows? It was the sins of mankind — my sins and your sins. To sympathize with Christ, then, is to appreciate the guilt, the malice, and the wormwood of sin. It means a realization of sin akin to Christ's apprehension of it. We must, as far as possible, feel as He felt toward it. We must strive to understand its black ingratitude and its effect upon His mind, heart, and body. We must try to see our sins in the bitter chalice which He drank. Thus only can we identify our sorrow with His sorrow. Without this true sympathy, our sorrow would be the mere spontaneous expression of natural emotion flowing from a source sharply and radically opposed to the inner and real source of Christ's sorrow.

Our Lord stressed this idea of sympathy when He exclaimed to the women of the Holy City, "Daughters of Jerusalem, weep not over me, but weep for yourselves and for your children."[36] Theirs was a natural sorrow occasioned by the sad plight to which suffering had reduced the Redeemer — only pity, inspired by the visible evidence of pain. He tried to fix

[36] Luke 23:28.

their minds on the real reason for His sorrow and suffering, which was their own hardness of heart and their sins, as well as the obstinacy and sins of the children yet to be born of them. He would bid them weep for Him only after they had wept for themselves, by directing their thoughts to the contemplation of the universal sorrow and affliction of mankind, so that, realizing and grieving over their own sins and those of their offspring, they might better understand what it cost Him to atone for them. A sorrowful realization of the effects of our sins, of their weight upon the heart of Christ, is absolutely necessary in order that our reflections on the Passion may redound to our spiritual welfare.

∞

Strive to see sin as Christ sees it

But this is not all. We must also strive to understand, as far as our finite minds can, the sensitiveness of Christ's pure and perfect nature.

No two individuals have the same moral perception of sin and the injury which it does to the God of infinite sanctity. The purity of our lives is the measure of our appreciation of the malice of sin. As we advance in virtue, we are more keenly sensitive to sin, more truly grieved over the consciousness of its commission.

And yet sin and its sad effects have never been novel, even to the holiest of us. We were born in sin. If we had ever been free from sin, if we could assume the personality of the unfallen Adam, only then might we have a truer idea of the perfect purity of Christ's nature. We cannot fully conceive what the hatefulness and the deformity of sin were to our first parents. We can, therefore, in no way understand the meaning of sin as Christ understood it, with His humanity substantially united by the tie of eternally indissoluble life with the Godhead. We must nonetheless try to deepen our realization of the perfect purity of Christ's nature, because, to understand His sorrow, we must grasp His estimate of sin and the sufferings which He underwent to expiate it.

We must also consider, in our meditation on the Passion, an unutterable mystery which calls rather for adoration than discussion. We must remember that the human and divine natures were substantially united in the person of Christ. Although these two natures are really distinct, there is, however, a bond of union between them, and consequently, a truth very difficult to understand, a oneness of consciousness and sympathy. What affected Christ's humanity touched mysteriously His very Godhead, so that, while He suffered as man, His Passion gripped His being as God, serving as an impetus to the manifestation of His eternal love which plunged Him into the depths of the sea and made the tempest overwhelm Him. "The waters are come in even unto my soul. I stick fast in the mire of the deep, and there is no sure standing. I am come into the depth of the sea, and a tempest hath overwhelmed me."[37]

∞

Understanding Christ's sacrifice
is the key to appreciating His love

In order that the Passion may draw us nearer to Christ, we must examine the idea of wholly disinterested love underlying

---

[37] Ps. 68:2-3 (RSV = Ps. 69:1-2).

it. Love has been so completely associated with selfishness, so closely bound up with some personal possession, so sharply severed from self-sacrifice, its touchstone and its law, that we cannot rise to the contemplation of the love that moved the Father to deliver His Son to the most agonizing of deaths and that urged the Son to surrender Himself to the will of the Father by utter self-oblation. We have no true notion of such love lavished upon beings of an immeasurably different and vastly inferior order of nature. We have but a very imperfect idea of the love of the saints for us, their brethren. How much more difficult to understand, how absolutely unfathomable is the love of God for His creatures — His sinful creatures! How marvelous that love which made Christ hide His divinity and die clothed in their fallen flesh!

To come to appreciate such love, we must soar on the wings of faith and seek a more accurate idea of sacrifice so immeasurable, of self-immolation so thorough, to which our minds are alien and which we can never repay. This idea of God's disinterested love is especially necessary in order that He may inspire us with a deeper knowledge of the reason which impelled Him to give Himself so unreservedly to ransom the doomed souls of men at the infinite price, with eternal pity that yearned to prove itself, even though it cost Him a life of sorrow and hardship unparalleled, a baptism in His blood.

How far beyond the intelligence even of the angels is this ineffable mystery of divine mercy, the true source of which is infinite, eternal love, which we will never fully understand! We may, however, if only through a glass in a dark manner, study Thy Revelation to us, O God, and reverently approach the everlasting hills from which Thou enlightenest wonderfully.

And in this bright sun of eternal love in which the saints find their endless bliss, and whose radiance dazzles and bewilders us, we may meditate on the Passion of Thy divine Son so that we may stand with great constancy and be numbered among the sons of God when He shall rise to judge.

While we follow Him along the Way of the Cross through the various stages of His sufferings, we should beseech the eternal Father to awaken in us an abiding consciousness of this momentous outpouring of divine love, a more loving response in our lives to its salutary lessons, and a more generous spirit of self-sacrifice for Him who "emptied Himself"[38] for us, that we may know only "Jesus Christ, and Him crucified."[39]

---

[38] Phil. 2:7.
[39] 1 Cor. 2:2.

Chapter Two

Make Heaven your goal

The idea of dying for man existed eternally in the mind of God. "Sacrifice and oblation thou didst not desire. . . . Burnt offering and sin offering thou didst not require. Then said I: Behold I come. In the head of the book it is written of me, that I should do Thy will: O my God, I have desired it, and Thy law in the midst of my heart."[40] Did not Holy Scripture teach us this truth? It follows from the fact that God is love, and the law of love is self-sacrifice.

Unlimited generosity characterizes all of God's dealings with His creatures. Creation, with its harmony, beauty, and grandeur, is the effect of God's disinterested love and infinite, eternal beneficence. It is an expression of a love that expects not even appreciation, much less a return, from its recipients. God manifested this love most signally to His creatures after man, in his arrogant pride and boastful self-sufficiency, had, by sin, struck ruthlessly at the majesty of his Maker, a jarring shock which upset the harmony of the divine plan and made the Creator curse the work of His hands.[41]

Christ was then to mount to the heights of self-extinction as the sacrifice by which He was to appease the wrath of the

[40] Ps. 39:7-9 (RSV = Ps. 40:6-8).
[41] Cf. Gen. 6:6.

Father. This free and unselfish oblation was to be developed by suffering and sorrow, and to be perfected by death. "God so loved the world as to give His only-begotten Son, that whosoever believeth in Him may not perish, but may have life everlasting."[42]

Accordingly, the Passion and death of Christ were to be the external expressions of what was most acceptable to the Father: the internal offering of Himself and His wholehearted obedience to the will of the Father.

In the Old Law, the completeness of the offering made the sacrifice perfect. The victim was entirely destroyed, the fire consuming it wholly. Thus did it symbolize the perfect self-surrender of a will identical — by its undivided obedience, by its absolute submission — with the will of God. Such was the nature of the sacrifice which Christ, clothed in our flesh, offered for us, and which we, united with Christ, can offer to the Father.

The true value of Christ's obedience to the will of the Father may be best measured by its prolific results. "As, by the disobedience of one man, many were made sinners, so also, by the obedience of one, many shall be made just."[43] Christ's obedience made His whole life a cross and a martyrdom. It was the soul of His sacrifice, affecting every part of His life and consummated on Calvary by His death. That death, which was the sinner's punishment, was accepted by the God-Man, because man, finite by nature, could not adequately atone for his sin.

[42] John 3:16.
[43] Rom. 5:19.

∞

Christ's sufferings increased as He advanced in age

To understand Christ's life of constant self-oblation, we must remember the distinction between the divine and human natures and, hence, between the divine and the human consciousness. Christ satisfied for man's sin because He was God as well as man, but He suffered as man. With the divine life, there can be "no change, nor shadow of alteration."[44] But Christ's human life was amenable to all the weaknesses of men, sin excepted. Just like us, Christ was subject to all the vicissitudes of frail humanity. As His human consciousness developed, His human knowledge increased. This is what the evangelist means when he says, "And Jesus advanced in wisdom and age and grace with God and men."[45] From the import of these words, it is clear that Christ really progressed in His acquired knowledge. It is not that the object of that knowledge was enlarged, but that many of the things which He knew from the beginning, either through His own divine knowledge or through the knowledge infused into Him by the Father, came, in a human way, within the scope of His human knowledge.

The full significance, then, of His future Passion and death gradually developed and expanded as Christ advanced in age. The heartaches, the weariness, the pain, the desolation; the sufferings of a refined nature exposed to the violence of coarse, unfeeling men; the sad plight of the Apostles; the sorrows of His Virgin Mother; and the awful sight of sin, its vileness, its

[44] James 1:17.
[45] Luke 2:52.

contempt, and its ingratitude — all this knowledge naturally unfolded itself to Christ's human intellect. As this knowledge increased, as its consciousness gradually sank in the depths of His human nature, the Redeemer was ever equal to the sacrifices demanded, yielding Himself to the terrible giving which they entailed as they progressively revealed themselves to His intelligence. Complete anticipation of suffering was, however, far different, even to Christ as man, from its actual realization. The actual experience of a trial transcends immeasurably any mental picture of it. So it was with Christ, who, regardless of His divine or His infused knowledge, was the Man of Sorrows. And consonant with the weaknesses of the creature to which He was subject, He grew and developed both mentally and physically.

Christ's human nature reached its full perfection at His Ascension. It was nonetheless perfect at every stage of its existence, but with a progressive perfection. The experimental knowledge which we obtain by degrees, Christ also acquired gradually. The more intensely He realized sorrow and suffering, the greater was His anguish and pain. The Gospel narrative exemplifies most definitely this gradual development. Thus, for instance, after Christ had gone about all the cities and towns, had taught in the synagogues, and had cured diverse diseases and infirmities, the realization of the people's distress, their dire need, and the woeful effects of their want of spiritual help suddenly touched the innermost spring of His pity and elicited from Him an expression of the sorrow that filled His heart and soul. "And seeing the multitude, He had compassion on them, because they were distressed and lying like sheep that have no shepherd. Then He said to His disciples: 'The harvest indeed is great, but the laborers are few. Pray ye therefore the Lord of the harvest, that He send forth laborers into His harvest.' "[46] The same progressive increase of suffering is seen in His words to the father of the lunatic child: "O unbelieving and perverse generation, how long shall I be with you? How long shall I suffer you?"[47]

This sudden manifestation of the gradually quickened sense of sorrow and pain was constantly evident in the Savior's dealings with the Apostles. He chided them on the Sea of Galilee for their lack of faith and confiding trust in His almighty power, when during the storm they cried out: "Lord, save us: we perish. And Jesus saith to them: 'Why are you fearful, O ye of little faith?' "[48] In the same way, when many of the disciples, having heard His solemn declaration, "Except you eat the flesh of the Son of Man, and drink His blood, you shall not have life in you," "walked no more with him"[49] — exclaiming, "How can this man give us His flesh to eat?" or, "This saying is hard, and who can hear it?"[50] — Christ turned to the Twelve and pleadingly expressed His sad feelings: "Will you also go away?"[51]

In His dealings with individuals, the full tide of human wickedness, vacillation, ignominy, outrage, cruelty, and contempt gradually flowed in upon His human consciousness. He

[46] Matt. 9:36-38.
[47] Matt. 17:16.
[48] Matt. 8:25-26.
[49] John 6:54, 67.
[50] John 6:53, 61.
[51] John 6:68.

beheld their sudden changes of feeling, their violent transitions from love to hatred, very clearly — when, for example, they followed Him into the desert under the spell of His divine magnetism and witnessed the miraculous multiplication of the loaves and fishes; when they brought to Him the sick and the maimed to be cured; when they cried out from their deepest souls: "Hosanna to the son of David. Blessed is He that cometh in the name of the Lord. Hosanna in the highest";[52] and, at the end of His temporal mission, when, steeled to the barbarity of Hell, many of them frantically shouted before Pilate: "Away with this man, and release unto us Barabbas."[53]

Although Christ knew all things, since He was God, His human intelligence realized only by degrees, in all their heartrending details, the full meaning of His utter rejection by His people and of the draining to the dregs the chalice of sorrow and suffering. As they loomed up before Him, His betrayal by Judas, one of the chosen Twelve, and His crucifixion between two outcasts must have caused Him far more intense anguish than the prevision of any other suffering.

The divine plan of the Redemption required this, since Christ, when He assumed our flesh, had to become like us in all things but sin. He had to suffer as man, and thus His human nature grew and developed according to the laws and conditions to which every created nature is subject. Throughout the gradual unfolding of His Passion, with the powers of Hell conspiring against Him, Christ experienced every affliction, every anxiety that we feel. His human nature was tremblingly

---

[52] Matt. 21:9.
[53] Luke 23:18.

responsive to love and hatred, to gentleness and violence, to kindness and contempt. He had to encounter sin in all its varied guises; and every nerve and fiber, keenly alive to the least touch of joy or sorrow, vibrated down to the utmost depths of His most delicately strung organism, far beyond the power of our coarse natures even to conceive, much less realize.

∞
Christ dedicated Himself to the Father's will

We must consider these facts so that we may better understand what Christ suffered even before His Passion actually began. Even before His Passion, He constantly yearned, as the knowledge of His sufferings revealed themselves to His mind, to consecrate Himself unreservedly to the accomplishment of His mission among men. This constant consecration of His human will to the divine will was visible in every act demanded by the economy of the Incarnation. Each sacrifice evoked from Christ's human soul a fixed resolve equal to the sacrifice required. All His human activity — mental, moral, and physical — every thought, word, and act, Christ subordinated to the great end of His earthly life: the Redemption of souls.

This continual giving of Himself to the gall and wormwood of His approaching sufferings and death — sorely tried so often by the countless exactions for self-sacrifice associated with His life of sorrow — Christ manifested on the night before He died. In His prayer for the Apostles, He exclaimed, "And for them do I sanctify myself."[54] Certainly Christ could

[54] John 17:19.

not sanctify Himself in the common meaning of the term, because He was the God of infinite sanctity. But the word *sanctify*, in this instance, signifies to set apart, to devote as an offering laid upon an altar. Christ was doing this inwardly when He uttered the words. He used the present tense to denote the continuity of the act. His Passion and death were to be the external expressions of this perennial self-oblation.

Interiorly, Christ was strengthening Himself, nerving His acutely tender sensibilities for the terrific conflict in which He was about to be engaged. His self-dedication to this one determination of His incarnate life was constant. But on special occasions He braced and intensified it. His vehement yearning for suffering had its climaxes, momentous indeed, like those rare crises in the lives of men, when souls marshal all their powers to meet difficulties or trials with grim earnestness and calm tenacity of purpose.

The Sacred Scriptures narrate many of these climaxes in our Lord's life. His experience in the Temple as a mere boy was one of them.[55] Spiritual writers state that this event prefigured Christ's future work and was an interior yearning, a consciously anticipated acceptance of it. The three days' loss symbolized the three years of sorrowful journeyings without one to comfort Him. His stay among the doctors marked His youthful consecration to the supreme work of His earthly career: His Father's business.

The temptation in the desert was still more significant as a preparation for the coming tragedy of suffering and death.[56] It

---

[55] Luke 2:46-49.
[56] Matt. 4:1-11; Mark 1:13; Luke 4:2-13.

was the mental prescience of the sorrowful struggle that Christ would wage to the bitter end. Spiritual conquest had to precede actual victory over the tempter. An inward triumph over all the emotions of His soul, their complete dedication to the will of the Father, had first to fortify His powers for the full assault of His Passion and death.

Christ, when bidden by the tempter to change stones into bread, chose to suffer rather than contravene the divine will. On the pinnacle of the Temple, the revelation of His miraculous power was placed in juxtaposition with His acceptance of the humble path of duty decreed for Him by His eternal Father, and Christ chose obedience to Him whose will was the meat by which He lived.[57] In the third temptation, the Savior preferred to establish His empire over the world by the Cross, by the utter extinction of Himself as man, by trampling underfoot all that man loves so ardently — the unstable and perishable belongings of fleeting time — rather than to acquire the material universe and its glory by yielding to the alluring seduction of riches, so subtly suggested by the father of lies.[58]

The temptation was, therefore, Christ's mental epitome of all the hardships that He would actually undergo even unto and including His death on the Cross. Christ, with perfect obedience, submitted to all the sad results of His sojourn among men, entirely accepting all the bitterness of His Passion, longing for the baptism of blood that He would undergo on Calvary.

[57] Cf. John 4:34.
[58] Cf. John 8:44.

∽

The vision of eternal glory
enabled Christ to bear His sufferings

The Transfiguration was another event in Christ's life closely associated with His sufferings and death. The mystery took place immediately after the Savior's first declaration of His Passion and death to the Apostles. "Then Jesus took unto Him the Twelve, and said to them, 'Behold, we go up to Jerusalem, and all things shall be accomplished which were written by the prophets concerning the Son of Man. For He shall be delivered to the Gentiles, and shall be mocked, and scourged, and spit upon; and after they have scourged Him, they will put Him to death, and the third day He shall rise again.' "[59] Then Christ asserts very explicitly the way to eternal glory with Him: "If any man will come after me, let him deny himself, and take up the Cross, and follow me. For he that will save his life shall lose it; and he that shall lose his life for my sake shall find it."[60] At once, Holy Scripture describes the Transfiguration: "And after six days, Jesus taketh unto Him Peter and James, and John his brother, and bringeth them up into a high mountain apart. And He was transfigured before them. And His face did shine as the sun, and His garments became white as snow."[61]

In this mystery, the closest connection is established between Christ's Passion and His eternal glory. By anticipation, the God-Man let the chosen three catch a glimpse of His humanity, as it would be forever — glorified. But this everlasting

---

[59] Luke 18:31-33.
[60] Matt. 16:24-25.
[61] Matt. 17:1-2.

reward was to be bought with His Passion and death. The brilliant light radiating from His body when "His face did shine as the sun" was the divine pledge to the disciples that "the sufferings of this time are not worthy to be compared with the glory to come, that shall be revealed in us."[62]

During the heavenly splendor of the Transfiguration, Moses and Elijah appeared and "spoke of His decease that He should accomplish in Jerusalem."[63] Christ yearned for His nerve-racking death on the Cross when He beheld the transcendent brightness of His earthly Transfiguration, which was a mere glimmering of the celestial glory destined for Him and His faithful followers.

In the mind of Christ, suffering and its eternal recompense were inseparably united. At certain periods of the Passion, they stirred His deepest consciousness. In Gethsemane, we observe Him instinctively recoil and swoon away, appalled and heartbroken, from the raging sea of man's sins, crying out, "My Father, if it be possible, let this chalice pass from me." Nonetheless, even when almost overwhelmed by the tempest, He immediately exclaims, "Not as I will, but as Thou wilt."[64]

The mental vision of eternal glory supported Christ throughout the course of His sufferings. This vision intensified, at times, into a longing for the agonizing death by which it was to be obtained: "I have a baptism wherewith I am to be baptized; and how I am straitened until it be accomplished!"[65]

---

[62] Rom. 8:18.

[63] Luke 9:31.

[64] Matt. 26:39.

[65] Cf. Luke 12:50.

∾

Christ is with you in your suffering

It is a truth taught us by Faith that union with Christ here is a prerequisite to union with Him forever: "Christ died for all, that they also who live may not now live to themselves, but unto Him who died for them and rose again."[66] The sanctification of our souls will effect this union, not only by making our souls holy and pleasing to God, but also by sanctifying them in the sense in which Christ sanctified Himself — consecrating, immolating them to Him on the altar of self-denial.

We have the same destiny as Christ. Our means of realizing it must be the same as His, for Christ is "the way, and the truth, and the life."[67] We must be one with Christ, because the nature that associates us with Him, although immeasurably inferior to His, is one with His, by reason of the personal union of the Savior's human nature with the Godhead. Hence, St. Paul says, "Let this mind be in you, which was also in Christ Jesus."[68] Recreated in Christ, we must be united with Him in the stress and storm of the struggle eternal in its issue. We must be one with Him in our progress in virtue, even though our sanctity can never equal His because we are finite beings.

This first eminently practical lesson we must weave into the fabric of our spiritual lives. The consideration that, despite our frailty, we are uniting ourselves with Christ — that His image is being formed in us by self-denial — should be a powerful impetus to urge us on in the battle for eternal life. This

---

[66] 2 Cor. 5:15.
[67] John 14:6.
[68] Phil. 2:5.

consideration should make us supremely confident that He is with us in the warfare between the cravings of the flesh and the strict, unyielding postulates of God's will. To realize our wondrous end, we must never forget that self-sacrifice is the fundamental law of the Christian life: "We are debtors, not to the flesh, to live according to the flesh. For if you live according to the flesh, you shall die; but if, by the Spirit, you mortify the deeds of the flesh, you shall live. . . . For the Spirit Himself giveth testimony to our spirit, that we are the sons of God. And if sons, heirs also; heirs indeed of God, and joint heirs with Christ . . . if we suffer with Him, that we may also be glorified with Him."[69] But, although the law of self-sacrifice is stern in its demands, although union with Christ means the bridling of weak nature — for "they that are Christ's, have crucified their flesh, with the vices and concupiscences"[70] — the consciousness of the bond of sympathy between us and our Savior will comfort and support us. What we suffer, Christ also has suffered. He has gone before us bearing His Cross: "The waters [of tribulation] are come in even unto my soul."[71]

∞

God calls you to self-sacrifice

In common with Christ, we have a work to do, an end to attain. During youth, the imagination creates for us a world in which we gladly live. It is a world of grandiose ideas and childish hopes, glowingly painted by an overwrought fancy,

[69] Rom. 8:12-13, 16-17.
[70] Gal. 5:24.
[71] Ps. 68:2 (RSV = Ps. 69:1).

beautifully colored by our natural desires. Often, these fanciful creations foreshadow future realities, but they are seldom realized as the imagination has depicted them. Too often, they are purely illusion and, like smoke, soon vanish from our mental horizon. Discovering the delusion, we wake suddenly from our daydreams, seized with the conviction that life and its duties are tangibly real, and we begin to live in the eternal now, making the actual present the forerunner of the near or distant future.

But sad indeed are the consequences of our early lethargy. How it has crippled the development of our spiritual strength which, all this time, would have steadily increased, had we grasped the palpable realities of life and cemented our union with God in virtue of our readier correspondence with grace!

God has created us to do a definite work for Him. To understand this truth, to realize that our lives are ordered by the infallible Providence of God and to live them in the light of this truth, is to attain the spiritual fruits of maturity. If we have lived too long as children, let us put away the toys of children during the remainder of life's probation, by trying better to appreciate the definiteness of our lives and hence, the particular duties of our lives and the self-denial involved in them. To do this is to draw nearer to God. The disappointment and dissatisfaction of many during life's exile are due to their failure to discharge the duties of their state in life. Fidelity to the work of our vocation will conform us completely to the divine will, uniting us with God now and forever.

Conformity to the divine will attacks our natural inclinations. It means wresting from the tenacious grasp of corrupt nature its inordinate attachment to objects, in themselves not sinful, but squaring with earthly rather than heavenly ideals. The price of such a sacrifice is strong endeavor and, at times, bitter pain. It requires us to snap asunder the link that binds us to earth, to forego self, to stifle the hankering after a life of luxury and ease, to ignore the din of fleeting popular applause, and to restrain our natural craving for a liberty that can easily degenerate into license. It requires us to make our wills docile to authority, to overthrow and pulverize the hydra-headed idol of self-sufficiency, self-opinionatedness, and the overweening desire to display, with pedantic passion, the conviction of our superior intelligence, and to cultivate a love for self-abasement. It requires us to be silent and peaceful under the lash of gross injustice, to be patient under the coarse treatment and contempt inflicted upon us through the hatred or the studied malice of men, and to moderate and suppress even reasonable sorrow. All of this costs us a strenuous effort — often, almost the crucifixion of our natural selves. And here it is a question, not of the gratification of sinful desires, but of the indulgence of that which is wholly lawful.

Is not the Cross, however, the direct antithesis of the satisfaction of even the legitimate impulses of nature? The grand characteristic of the Passion, in all its unspeakable rigor, was the manliness of the God-Man. Christ was neither weak nor soft, for He yearned for suffering. He has given us the example. "For this is thankworthy, if, for conscience toward God, a man endures sorrows, suffering wrongfully. For what glory is it, if committing sin, and being buffeted for it, you endure? But if, doing well, you suffer patiently, this is thankworthy before God. For unto this are you called, because Christ also suffered for us, leaving you an example that you should follow His steps."[72] To follow Christ, self-sacrifice must be the guiding principle of our lives. The flesh must be subdued, mastered. With fixed resoluteness of will, we must grapple with and conquer the disorders of unmortified nature, offering them up to Christ who, "having joy set before Him, endured the Cross, despising the shame."[73]

∞

Contemplating Heaven will
sustain you in your sufferings

The soul in its moral struggle, in its life of self-sacrifice, will sustain itself by looking beyond and contemplating its eternal reward. The horizon of this life, upon which the vision of so many is too intensely focused, blinds them to the true life hereafter. Hereafter is the eternal reality. Hereafter is the answer to the contradictions of earth, the interpretation and the finality of the dispensations of God's Providence. Hereafter is the light, "the true light, which enlighteneth every man that cometh into this world."[74] It is the light that illumines our minds and directs "our feet into the way of peace"[75] amid the turmoil of life. It is the light that pierces and dispels the black, lowering clouds of doubt and the mists of uncertainty that obscure the path of the distressed traveler journeying toward the eternal court of the Lord. Hereafter is the eternal enjoyment of our temporal yearning. Hereafter is the joy that lightens

[72] 1 Pet. 2:19-21.
[73] Heb. 12:2.
[74] John 1:9.
[75] Luke 1:79.

life's burden and tempers the bitterness of suffering, the "joy no man shall take from you."[76]

Realizing this, we will "pursue justice, godliness, faith, charity, patience, mildness."[77] We will "fight the good fight of faith" and "lay hold on eternal life,"[78] to which we are called, by running "the way of God's commandments,"[79] by leading lives of love. We will accomplish this by joyously accepting the self-sacrifice essential to such lives, uniting ourselves heart and soul with Christ, the Man of Sorrows, with the infallible assurance that "this slight momentary affliction is preparing us for an eternal weight of glory beyond all comparison."[80]

---

[76] John 16:22.

[77] 1 Tim. 6:11.

[78] 1 Tim. 6:12.

[79] Cf. Ps. 118:32 (RSV = Ps. 119:32).

[80] 2 Cor. 4:17.

Chapter Three

∞

*Strive to conquer
your self-will*

Throughout the varied sufferings of His Passion, amid the implacable envy and the intense hatred of a savagely ferocious, bloodthirsty populace, Christ ever yearned to accomplish His mission of dying for man. Solitary and alone, for none could fathom the depths of His desolation, and without sympathy, for none could realize the pain underlying the emotions of His gentle soul, Christ, with cool gravity, with exemplary patience, and with calm composure of countenance, never faltered in the work eternally efficacious for sinners.

But at times, like a mighty river swelling and overflowing its banks, the Savior's infinitely strong feelings rose to the surface and suffused His features with the struggling sensations raging within Him. After His triumphal entrance into Jerusalem, Christ gave open expression to His interior conflict. "Now is my soul troubled. And what shall I say: Father, save me from this hour? But for this cause I came unto this hour."[81]

This access to the Redeemer's afflicted and heavily laden soul should help us to understand the most acute pain, the keenest distress, that Christ felt beneath the serenity of His soul. It should explain the agony in Gethsemane, in which He sank almost overwhelmed, when the appalling, sickening

---

[81] John 12:27.

sight of man's sins forced the blood from every pore of His sacred body.

∞

Christ suffered His Passion throughout His life

The Passion is too often inaccurately associated only with Christ's last sufferings. The Savior was the Man of Sorrows all His life. The trials of His childhood; His exile in Egypt; the taunts of His enemies, their vindictiveness, their attempts on His life; the caustic contempt for Him everywhere; the vacillation of the disciples, their dullness of understanding, their coarseness; the sin and disease confronting Him constantly; the disorder wrought by sin, with its effect upon His refined, sensitively responsive nature — all these causes of untold anguish to Christ we hardly consider. The God-Man seems to do the same, for, predicting His death and its concomitant sorrows, He says that Elijah has already come, "and they knew him not, but have done unto him whatsoever they had a mind. So also the Son of Man shall suffer from them."[82] He foregoes the past and the present and speaks only of His future sufferings.

These words conceal a deep truth. Beyond doubt, the sufferings at the end of Christ's life were more rigorous, for only then was He "delivered to the Gentiles and . . . mocked, and scourged, and spit upon,"[83] and this surely was a new form of suffering. Then, indeed, was He most forsaken by all. Judas betrayed Him, Peter denied Him, and the Apostles fled from

[82] Matt. 17:12.
[83] Luke 18:32.

Him. But these facts cannot explain the striking contrast in the language of Holy Scripture. The peculiar characteristics of the last sufferings consist in this: they reveal the inward agony of the innocent Lamb of God, led like "a sheep to the slaughter."[84] At the close of Christ's life, the black cloud overshadowing Him all His days became blacker; the burden of sin weighed more heavily upon Him; the realization of the Father's hatred of sin was intensified; and the thought of the eternal death of man because of sin cut into His heart.

The very beginning of the twenty-sixth chapter of St. Matthew marks a sudden transition in the narrative. It vividly paints this particular and unique period of suffering. The evangelist describes a momentously important phase of Christ's life. "And it came to pass, when Jesus had ended all these words, He said to His disciples, 'You know that after two days shall be the Pasch, and the Son of Man shall be delivered up to be crucified.' "[85] Here the history of the Passion begins, and it is the subject of the rest of the Gospel.

The Passion may be divided into two parts. The first began with the Last Supper and closed with the agony. The other commenced with Christ's apprehension after the agony and ended with His death. There is a notable difference between them. The first was characterized by an unearthly tranquillity visible on Christ's countenance despite the storm agitating His soul. The second was distinguished by unspeakable suffering from without — Christ yielding Himself completely to the inhuman brutality of His enemies — but undisturbed

[84] Isa. 53:7.
[85] Matt. 26:1-2.

peace reigned within, except during the three hours' agony when He was almost wholly submerged by the overflowing sea of sorrow.

∞

The coming betrayal saddened
Christ during the Last Supper

The most touchingly beautiful incident of the first period was the institution of the Holy Eucharist — the Savior giving Himself, body and blood, soul and divinity, as a pledge of immortality to man. With a minuteness of detail, Christ bade the Apostles to prepare for the Last Supper. He sat down and waited upon them. "And whilst they were eating, Jesus took bread and, blessing, broke and gave to them and said, 'Take ye. This is my body.' And having taken the chalice, giving thanks, He gave it to them. And they all drank of it. And He said to them, 'This is my blood of the new testament, which shall be shed for many.' "[86] It was the practical representation of the great sacrifice which He would offer on the morrow, the vivid anticipation of the final dereliction of His Passion.

During this most munificent giving of Himself, Christ felt the first violent attack of the bitter anguish of His Passion. His soul was transfixed by the realization of His betrayal by one of His own intimate associates. It was the assault of Hell upon His finest sensibilities, the deadly contagion of sin within the circle of those whom He had guarded so carefully, taught so solicitously, and loved so ardently. It was the powers of Hell gloating triumphantly over the moral shipwreck of him whom

[86] Mark 14:22-24.

He had chosen from eternity to be His apostle. Not resentment, but love disappointed in its longing to reclaim the recreant apostle, greatly depressed Him — infinite yearning forced to yield to infinite sorrow for the lost soul of the traitor.

To be betrayed by one of the Twelve, His friend, His apostle, His priest — this it was that cut so deeply the eternal Lover of men. "If my enemy had reviled me, I would verily have borne with it. And if he that hated me had spoken great things against me, I would perhaps have hidden myself from him. But thou, a man of one mind, my guide, and my familiar, who didst take sweetmeats together with me, in the house of God, we walked with consent."[87] This was the veil that hung like a pall over the marvelous manifestation of love that He was enacting in the midst of them. The flood tide of Christ's distress at length rose and freely overflowed in words of bitter sorrow: "And whilst they were eating, He said, 'Amen, I say to you that one of you is about to betray me. . . . Woe to that man by whom the Son of Man shall be betrayed.' "[88] "You are clean, but not all."[89] "The hand of him that betrayeth me is with me on the table."[90] These are the sad expressions of an eternal love that had called to the priesthood an apostle who was now about to make Him the victim of his hypocrisy and the sport of a treachery inspired by the duplicity of Hell.

But just at that very moment, Christ's intense desire to immolate Himself for man, and His joy at the thought of His

---

[87] Ps. 54:13-15 (RSV = Ps. 55:12-14).
[88] Matt. 26:21, 24.
[89] John 13:10.
[90] Luke 22:21.

victory over the powers of darkness, deepened by the eternal glory purchased for souls by His death, received renewed momentum. This exulting joy clamored for utterance and revealed itself with greater vigor when Judas left the Cenacle.[91] "When he therefore was gone out, Jesus said, 'Now is the Son of Man glorified, and God is glorified in Him. If God be glorified in Him, God also will glorify Him in Himself; and immediately will He glorify him.' "[92] Then follows a discourse divinely eloquent on the effect of His Passion now begun. From the depths of His being, the great High Priest pleads with peculiar energy and intensified ardor to ransom souls, soaring, in His infinite love for them, far above the harrowing suffering by which it was to be accomplished. This was the last joyous anticipation of triumph before the Crucifixion.

∞

In His agony, Christ experienced
the crucifixion of His soul

The door of the Cenacle closed upon Him and His disciples, and they proceeded through the valley of Jehoshaphat, over the brook of Cedron, and entered Gethsemane. There is a sorrowful silence that touches us to tears as the God-Man journeys to the scene of His fearful struggle with death. As He approaches the garden in the silent solitude of the night, mentally experiencing His heart-rending agony, He suppresses the secret shuddering of His human soul, as the groans of death and the powers of Hell surround Him and attack His deepest

---

[91] The Cenacle, or eating room, was the site of the Last Supper.
[92] John 13:31-32.

source of life. Despite His distinct anticipation of His Passion and His ardent yearning to die for souls, He now sinks to earth with a broken heart, almost crushed by the oppressive weight of the sins of humanity, seized by the agony of death.

Christ was true God and true man. But the Godhead super-added nothing to what the manhood possessed as a created nature. Although one in personality, the two natures in Christ were really distinct. When He assumed our flesh, He therefore bound Himself to all the laws incident to human nature. He became like us in all things but sin. He was subject to every infirmity to which we are heir. The Godhead did not change or diminish the rigor of His sufferings in the least. The agony was the searching sorrow and the acute anguish of Christ's manhood, which alone could suffer and die. The only effect of the Godhead upon the manhood was to increase its pain by indescribably refining Christ's human nature.

Most graphic is the language that portrays the struggle that convulsed Christ in Gethsemane. St. Mark states, "He began to fear."[93] It was the fear of one transfixed with terror at the sight of an object that paralyzes its beholder with overpowering horror, shaking the innermost seat of life. "And," continues the evangelist, "to be heavy." It was excessive sorrow shriveling the vital activities of His soul, exhausting and atrophying the most hidden spring of His physical being. St. Luke speaks of Christ's being "in an agony," that is, overcome by intense fear, writhing in a terrific struggle with a powerful foe. "And being in an agony, He prayed the longer,"[94] or with

[93] Mark 14:33.
[94] Luke 22:43.

persevering insistence, with greater earnestness, for immediate comfort, and for an end to the sorrow in the utmost depths of His desolation.

Holy Scripture depicts our Lord's actions during this memorable scene, and they harmonize perfectly with the words that describe the interior conflict and distressing convulsions of His sensitive soul. He leans on Peter, James, and John, longing for them to be near Him, to console Him in the extremity of His excruciating suffering. Then He is "withdrawn away from them";[95] the original word, meaning rent, or torn away by force, from the chosen three, is much stronger. He proceeds further into the garden and, falling on His knees, prays. Finally, He returns to the disciples, only to find them fast asleep, faithless to their duty. He goes to pray, and returns to them again and again. These nervous movements in quest of solace and sympathy are a true but a very faint picture of the anguish and the desolation within His heavily burdened, horror-stricken soul. His prayer — "Father, if Thou wilt, remove this chalice from me; but yet not my will, but Thine be done"[96] — eloquently describes the same storm of convulsed emotions: the thought of relief, only to be frustrated; the weak human nature shrinking away terrorized, but strengthened for the conflict by its union with the divine nature; the frail body hungering for rest from sorrow, but checked in its desire by complete conformity to the divine will. "Not my will, but Thine be done."

O God-Man in agony, these furious convulsions, this withering suffering and sorrow that so afflicted Thy soul, this

---

[95] Luke 22:41.
[96] Luke 22:42.

intolerable weight that crushed Thee to the earth, this restless anguish, this paralyzing fear — what was the cause of it all? It was not that Thou didst lose sight of Thy Father's will or had ever failed to obey Him most docilely. It was not weak human nature so overpowering Thee as to make Thee prefer, had it accorded with the plan of Redemption, a diminution of sorrow and suffering. It was not the powers of Hell striking terror into Thy soul, overwhelming Thee with heartbreaking grief in order to make Thee more completely one with us in our afflictions. It was not the fear of death, for death, however shameful and cruel, could not annihilate Thy divine nature. Besides, O King of martyrs, Thou wouldst not fear what they so cheerfully and so lovingly embraced. Was it the anger of Thy Father smiting Thee? Thou and Thy Father were one, and Thou wast constantly conscious of the eternally inseparable union. Was it the sinner's sense of sin that so burdened Thee? It would be blasphemous to assert that the sinner's consciousness of sin and Thine were identical. Thou, O God of infinite sanctity, couldst not sin. Sin was man's, but its awful punishment was Thine. "For the wickedness of my people have I struck him."[97] The realization of the transcendent malice of sin and the infinite price of its expiation were, O Christ, the reasons for Thy soul-stirring agony.

All these diverse torments were the bitter ingredients of that mental sorrow that bathed the Redeemer in His blood, of that deluge of desolation that flooded the human soul of Christ in His mortal agony. He was, in the garden, assuming the gigantic load of the sins of the flesh with which He had

---

[97] Isa. 53:8.

clothed Himself, experiencing the terrors of death as their punishment and accepting the almighty vengeance of His outraged Father as their final eternal curse. Christ carried in Gethsemane the burden of sins and bore their chastisement as if He were guilty of them all, and not their innocent victim. He fully grasped the enormity of man's sins, their multiplicity, their degradation, and the immeasurable suffering about to be inflicted upon Him by His creatures because of them. In His deepest consciousness, He beheld the sinner's eternal punishment, and this was the crucifixion of His gentle, sensitive soul — incomparably more painful than the crucifixion of His bruised and battered body.

At the very climax of Christ's agony, when the sweat of blood crimsoned Him from head to foot, an angel appeared, to strengthen Him.[98] Is it possible that the eternal God could be strengthened by His own creature? He is the God of infinite strength, "upholding all things by the word of His power."[99] He is the fullness of life: "Of Him, and by Him, and in Him are all things."[100] The creature could not give Him what He already possessed in its plenitude. Christ, in His agony, permitted His glorious human soul to be so overpowered, to be so helpless, as to need sympathy and support from His weak creature; or perhaps the angel's appearance was the pledge of the eternal glory that would inevitably follow His Passion and death, the dim glimmering, the feeble anticipation of the Father's everlasting reward. This presence of the angel energized Christ's soul with

[98] Luke 22:43-44.
[99] Heb. 1:3.
[100] Rom. 11:36.

strength far more amazing than that which had been almost annihilated within Him in His mighty battle with death.

Renewed in spirit, and fortified by absolute surrender to the will of the Father, Christ rose after His inconceivable agony. There is an air of restored calm in His words to the apostles: "Rise, let us go."[101] As He is about to become the victim of the most cruelly revolting violence that will end when the sword goes quivering through His Sacred Heart, His serene countenance bespeaks His peace of soul.

∞

God calls you to conquer your inferior will

From Christ's agony, we can learn a lesson replete with the most sublime sanctity. As in our own, so in Christ's human nature, there is a twofold inclination of the will: the higher, or nobler, inclination nearly identical with the divine will, and the other, although distinct from it, nonetheless united with it by complete resignation. The human will of Christ was ever one with the divine will. But this does not prove that His loving giving of Himself to all the torments of His Passion demanded no effort or cost Him no pain.

His finely sensitive human soul unconsciously shrinking from suffering; the intense desire to be relieved of the oppressive burden of man's sins; the cry of unfathomable sorrow to the Father to let the bitter chalice pass from Him; the longing for sympathy from the apostles, despite its impossibility — these were the indeliberate impulses of the human will constantly mounting higher in hopes of acquiring rest. They

---

[101] Matt. 26:46.

formed the strength of the inferior inclination, the *self* ever extinguished which Christ felt in all His pain. Our Lord spoke to the Apostles of the perseverance of His trials: "You are they who have continued with me in my temptations."[102] The Savior was sorely tried all His life; His inferior will, repeatedly denied and conquered, was wholly immolated for us on the Cross.

We must read aright and learn, according to our ability, the lesson from the amazing suffering and endurance of a nature the very same as ours. Even when we have mastered the flesh and its sordid appetite, we experience the war of the body against the soul, and to be victorious in this means, at times, anguish supreme. Although our self-denial may be all-embracing, although our consecration to God may be wholehearted, our tendency is to follow the easier course and to spare ourselves in the conflict. Succeeding this tendency is the strong desire. Then we listen to the tempter. Next, our spiritual vision becomes faint; our fixed resolution begins to weaken and waver under the realization of our frailty, the gloom of doubt, and the cloud of magnified fears in which we discern, even with our impaired spiritual sight, far greater sacrifice than we had anticipated. And oh, how weary and wearing is the struggle! In a severely distressing experience like this, we can answer that most momentous of all questions: Are we Christ's?

If we are to be Christ's in life and in death, habitual self-renunciation is essential. We cannot crucify our flesh, with the vices and concupiscences,[103] we cannot "mortify the deeds

---

[102] Luke 22:28.
[103] Cf. Gal. 5:24.

of the flesh,"[104] unless we perseveringly forego self. The will of God must, then, so influence us that our baser selves are ever subject to it, submitting entirely to its sovereign sway, even if it costs us life itself.

An examination of the past may reveal the reign of passion — vehement desires, their full satisfaction, an absolute lack of self-control. For the future, we must be docile, ever ready to yield to the least bidding of the divine will, the flesh ever subject to the spirit, our natural selves forced to rise above visible things to the contemplation of the glory yet unseen, but tenaciously grasped as the infinite reward of daily self-sacrifice, and the sorrow, anguish, disappointments, heartaches, and desolation of such a life.

To accept our cross cheerfully should be our one aim. Strengthened with the strength of God, and fighting courageously, we will conquer in the struggle with our natural inclinations. A prolific source of discouragement will be strong emotions, followed by grave fears created by a too-active imagination, which will magnify real or fancied difficulties, intensify the yearning to deepen the wound inflicted by self-love, and insistently recall to sickening satiety the fear, the hardship, and the loss. These are the doors through which the Devil enters and strives to gain complete possession of the soul. Then the interior light grows dim, and the soul's vision wrought by faith is clouded. In this darkness, doubts at once arise about the value of the supernatural, the necessity of grace, the presence in the soul of the Triune God, and His goodness and great love — doubts which waste the soul's

[104] Rom. 8:13.

strength, robbing it of peace, neutralizing the effects of its self-denial, crushing its efforts, and paralyzing all its powers by throwing it into a turmoil of unrest. Thus the noble will succumbs, and pride and sensuality seize the soul in triumph.

∞

Seek union with Christ through
conformity with God's will

The great remedy against such falls, the life of spiritual progress, must be sought in the control we exercise over the tendencies of the will in attuning them to the Presence so intimate to each of us in the performance of our very ordinary duties. In rising promptly, in consecrating the first fruits of the day to God, in preparing our soul for its combat with the world, in perfect self-possession during social interchanges, in patience under the stress of unexpected and very trying annoyances, in tranquillity of manner amid innumerable interactions and continual labor, in habitual self-denial in the government of our thoughts and our actions, in daily self-suppression, especially on the occasions of sudden surprises which test the temper of soul — in these ways, the higher will can assert its absolute dominion. As grace gains the ascendancy through these victories, God's reign within the soul becomes permanent, filling the soul with heavenly peace, nerving it for future victories, and preparing it for eternal union with Christ as the reward for its conformity to the divine will.

These repeated conquests, through God's help, increase the spiritual vigor of the will, thus disposing the soul for the loving acceptance of harder sacrifices and assuring it of final victory. This majestic mastery of our lower selves purifies the mind, clarifies the vision of the unseen, and deepens our appreciation of the substantial reality of religious truth. The soul formed in the school of self-discipline, in which inferior nature is subdued, beholds the future bright and beautiful, and is sustained by the conviction that "the sufferings of this time are not worthy to be compared with the glory to come,"[105] for moral death to self will finally issue in union with Christ forever.

---

[105] Rom. 8:18.

Chapter Four

∞

Perfect your love
by uniting your sufferings
with Christ's

∞

We cannot meditate on Christ's Passion without considering His unspeakable love. Suffering and love are so intimately associated that they cannot be divorced. The sensibilities of love measure the acuteness of pain. The man who loves but little feels but little pain. As the severity of bodily suffering depends upon mental consciousness, so the keenness of mental anguish depends upon the fineness of the sensibilities or the feelings.

Love wounded by an injury is vastly different from the mere perception of it. The heart may be crushed within a man who loves ardently when he perceives an act of unkindness on the part of the object of his love, whereas the mere contemplation of such an act impresses but little when the sensibilities of love are not wounded by it. The source of mental suffering is far deeper than the apprehension of it. The pagans were prompted by one of the deepest, noblest impulses and finest instincts of humanity to exclaim of the Christians: "Behold how they love one another."[106]

Moreover, the finer the nature, the more sensitive are the feelings. The man who rises above selfishness, who is not

---

[106] Cf. Tertullian (c. 160-225; African Church Father), *Apology*, ch. 39, sect. 7.

chained to earth by the earthly, whose fiber is delicate and fine, feels suffering much more intensely than the man of coarse nature who is guided by low, sordid motives.

The word *love* does not, however, fully define the deep-rooted spring of acute sensibility. Love has been defined as "the drawing of one being to another with a strong desire for union and rest in that union." But this is only one element of sensibility. There is also a form of sensibility called benevolence, which is the lavishing of self upon others without the personal feelings essential to love. Charity or benevolence identified with tenderness, and compassion born of sympathy, pain, and fear are likewise two distinct phases of sensibility, but they are not the same as the principle itself. Sensibility is as deep and as strong and as broad as life. It is dearer than life, because love will sacrifice life before life will forego love.

The principle of sensibility springs from the depths of the heart. "Love," says Holy Scripture, "is strong as death."[107] The term *love*, although unable to convey the full meaning of this interior vital principle, since it is only its finest, purest, and most attractive offspring, is nonetheless the most accurate word to describe the inner source of the heart's emotions.

The love of the saints we can but faintly grasp. More feeble still is our comprehension of the height and depth, the length and breadth of God's love, but we find the highest development, the grandest expression of all human love, in Christ. The characteristic virtue of His humanity, the soul of His activity, the freest, most munificent effect of His manhood was love. Here, however, we will consider only a particular aspect

---

[107] Cant. 8:6 (RSV = Song of Sol. 8:6).

of Christ's love: its encounter with sin and its actual yearning to conquer it.

∞

Before His Passion, Christ
poured forth the sufferings of His heart

There is a striking difference between Christ's love during the Passion and His love during the early period of His life. Before His Passion, the Savior poured forth His holy zeal and righteous indignation against those who had disappointed or wounded His love by sin. He denounced the Pharisees with startling words for their duplicity, their hardness of heart, and their treacherously hostile opposition to His teaching: "Woe to you scribes and Pharisees, hypocrites: because you make clean the outside of the cup and of the dish, but within you are full of rapine and uncleanness. Thou blind Pharisee, first make clean the inside of the cup and of the dish, that the outside may become clean. Woe to you scribes and Pharisees, hypocrites, because you are like whited sepulchers, which outwardly appear to men beautiful, but within are full of dead men's bones, and of all filthiness. So you also outwardly indeed appear to men just, but inwardly you are full of hypocrisy and iniquity. . . . You serpents, generation of vipers, how will you flee from the judgment of Hell?"[108]

These are the outbursts of the suffering of a heart bitterly distressed by the sinner's rejection of grace. They are the manifestation of a love defeated in its supreme effort to console and bless. They are an unsparing denunciation of the malice of

[108] Matt. 23:25-28, 33.

sin and an eternal longing to efface it, save the sinner, and reveal the awesome sanctity and the inexorable justice of God. Even the Apostles, when unintentionally not conformed to the divine will, were not spared Christ's burning zeal and acute sensibility. He reprimanded St. Peter when, with all the ardor of his sincerity, he would have opposed His death: "Go behind me, Satan; thou art a scandal unto me, because thou savorest not the things that are of God, but the things that are of men."[109] Referring to the traitor, He said, "One of you is a devil."[110]

During His Passion, Christ suffered in gentle silence
But, during the Passion, love spoke no longer in anger. Its zeal strove not to restrain the wickedness of man. The deeply wounded heart of Christ allowed itself to be transfigured by the sins of humanity without complaining or manifesting its secret horror at the thought of the sinner's eternal curse. Man had so steeled himself against the beneficent influence of divine love as not to heed its wondrous appeal. The personal sorrow at the sight of sin, which swelled into almighty indignation and vented its wrath in words of uncompromising reproof, has spent itself. The voice of solemn warning and of searing denunciation of sin, flowing from the realization of the insult that it offered to the eternal Father, is now silent. Sin in all its hideous reality holds triumphant sway, and now only plaintively heard is the pleading cry of love welling up in the

---

[109] Matt. 16:23.
[110] John 6:71.

bleeding and broken heart, apparently overcome by sin, but yearning to eradicate it — the sorrowful wail of the grief-stricken soul seeking only to reclaim those about to redden their hands in the blood of their God.

To Judas, Christ speaks in the accents of the tenderest love, exclaiming, "Friend, whereto art thou come?"[111] He asks a soldier to free one of His hands that He may touch and heal the ear of Malchus.[112] The most intense love, mingled with unfathomable sorrow, emanates from His eyes glancing at Peter after the boastful apostle's denial of his Master.[113] Infinite patience and ineffable meekness are His only answer to the brutal soldier who struck and staggered Him by the force of his blow: "If I have spoken evil, give testimony of the evil; but if well, why strikest thou me?"[114] When He reproaches the women of Jerusalem, it is with words of unutterable love and poignant grief: "Daughters of Jerusalem, weep not over me, but weep for yourselves and for your children."[115] Even when spit upon, Jesus was silent.

Christ's soul-piercing lament over the Holy City marked the tenderly touching change in the movement of His love: "Jerusalem, Jerusalem, thou that killest the prophets and stonest them that are sent unto thee, how often would I have gathered together thy children, as the hen doth gather her chickens under her wings, and thou wouldst not! Behold, your house

[111] Matt. 26:50.
[112] Cf. Luke 22:50-51; John 18:10.
[113] Luke 22:60-61.
[114] John 18:23.
[115] Luke 23:28.

shall be left to you desolate."[116] These words are the last effort of grace, the final endeavor of one form of love "to seek and to save that which was lost."[117]

Love now reveals itself far differently. Christ's public life, marked by untold ingratitude and replete with constant labor, and heartfelt yearning to save the sinner, had swiftly passed, and the sword of keen regret for love spurned and grace abused had riven His divine heart. The Redeemer now struggles no longer with sin, but gives Himself unreservedly to suffer the last tortures of His Passion. Love now speaks only when there is a loving response from its recipients. And yet, the most signal manifestation of Christ's love came from the Cross.

The deepest expressions of divine love are Christ's seven last words, the most momentous ever uttered by man in the agony of death.

The first word spoken by Christ while He was being brutally nailed to the Cross, "Father, forgive them, for they know not what they do,"[118] illustrates His undying love for His bitterest enemies in the very act of crucifying Him. The second word, "Amen, I say to thee, this day thou shalt be with me in Paradise,"[119] manifests His mercy to sinners, and the desire that burned within Him to draw them to Himself both for time and for eternity. The third word, "Woman, behold thy son,"[120] breathes His infinite solicitude for souls by lavishing

[116] Matt. 23:37-38.
[117] Luke 19:10.
[118] Luke 23:34.
[119] Luke 23:43.
[120] John 19:26.

upon them His Mother to be their mother, and so guard His dearest interests.

Love mounts still higher as the last agony approaches. "My God, my God, why hast Thou forsaken me?"[121] tells of Christ's dereliction of soul, so that He might be most intimately united with sinners in the overpowering lonely desolation of their abandoned state. "I thirst"[122] goes beyond His bodily sufferings into the finest fibers of His divinely sensitive soul, describing a thirst such as only Christ could have for the salvation of men and the consequent glory of His Father. "It is consummated"[123] is the expression of the gratitude of love that, by His death, eternal joy had been purchased for His creatures. And the last word, "Father, into Thy hands I commend my spirit,"[124] is love returning whence it came, an eternal union of the love of Christ with the love of the Father, the Holy Spirit, and redeemed souls abiding in their true home, the bosom of the Triune God.

∞

Suffering is bound up with love

Christ's Passion exemplifies the laws necessary for an ideal life in man. The grandest types of manhood or of womanhood are those in which love and suffering are interwoven — love being the essence of life, the spring of its action; and suffering being the purifying, refining element of love. The beauty of

[121] Matt. 27:46.
[122] John 19:28.
[123] John 19:30.
[124] Luke 23:46.

such characters indelibly stamps itself upon our memories, captivates our minds and our hearts, and inspires us with lasting reverence. The greatness whose dominant note is love casts the most magic spell, wields the most powerful influence over us.

But love without pain has never risen to the heights of true greatness and moral grandeur. The mind can think of nothing more wonderful than Christ suffering and humiliated to the dust for us sinners. Yet Christ, in becoming the Man of Sorrows, mirrors for us the highest ideal of true greatness — the ideal that sounds the very depths of human sympathy: the blending of suffering with love.

Christ's death accomplished two ends. It satisfied the eternal Father for man's sin, and it raised man from the lowest level of moral degradation to the apex of moral nobility. To effect this latter end, suffering was the law decreed by God and hence, the purifying process of human nature for its elevation to an ideal life. The Son of God, therefore, in assuming flesh, had to live according to the laws of man's nature. He could not be other than human.

Just as in Christ, so necessarily in every human soul, suffering and love must be the established law of the soul's life, perfecting the soul by conforming it to the divine Model and thus preparing it for eternal union with God.

∞

Accept suffering without
complaining or growing despondent

For suffering so to transfigure the soul, the soul must accept it with resignation to the divine will and not hinder its salutary, chastening influence by yielding to the two natural evils that follow in its wake.

The first is an inclination to fret and to complain. As a spirited horse, quickly checked by a skillful driver, trembles in every limb and strives furiously to free itself from the hand that restrains it, so love, meeting an unexpected check, changes into violent rage, imagining injustice, injury, and contempt where none whatsoever exist — all as a result of love's selfishness. Thus thwarted, where, perhaps, it hoped most for a return of sympathy and kindness, love is forced in upon itself. The finest emotions and the purest instincts of the heart are either blighted and wither away or yield to bitter complaints, making all that is fair and beautiful, foul and ugly. The soul in this state attacks even God Himself — murmuring at least against His want of consideration, if not His cruelty — questions the dispensations of His unerring Providence, or imagines that evil has finally triumphed over good — has even conquered God.

Another evil that often coexists with suffering is despondency. The soul is thrown back on itself, brooding over the sense that its truest and most sublime impulses are wasted upon a cruel, unfeeling world. Tortured by imaginary wrongs, the soul foregoes its ideals, loses faith in manhood's or womanhood's foremost characters, becomes morbidly introspective, creates innumerable fanciful heroes, or chafes and sighs because it cannot realize the dreams of its abnormal imagination. This oversensitiveness deceives the soul's sincerest and finest emotions and begets a proud self-sufficiency whose deadly virus poisons the soul with the idea of a supposed exaltation above the rest of humanity, and saddens the soul beyond words with the thought that, since it is so incomparably superior to all others, there can be on earth no response to the nobility of its aspirations and, therefore, no real ground of sympathy with them.

∞

Suffering will make your love soar highest

The lessons taught by the Passion will dispel these two evils. The Passion teaches us that suffering of every description — all the physical and moral agony of the human heart, blind submission to the will of God, daily self-denial, constant self-sacrifice — are the agencies that refine and make love soar highest. The realization of love's most cherished hopes is very desirable, but the refinement of love through being misunderstood, through bitter disappointment, through soul-stirring anguish, is immeasurably more desirable. The divesting love of selfishness, the robbing it of any earthly element, is preferable to its transitory satisfaction.

The Passion also teaches us that love restrained in one direction may attain its best exercise in another. Christ found an outlet for His love in channels not always sought by Him. So, too, may we. We are not all called to prove our love by martyrdom, but we can manifest it by the patient endurance of the cross that God sends us. We may not be able, with our earthly store, to put an end to poverty and to dissipate destitution, but we can diffuse "the good odor of Christ"[125] by kindness in word and act, and thus help to lighten the burden of pain and sorrow oppressing the hearts of our fellowmen. Our love may be

[125] 2 Cor. 2:15.

checked and defeated, our noble projects and unselfish aims may be scoffed at, even ridiculed, but let us commend all to God, and let Him accomplish the realization of our heartfelt yearning as it shall please Him. According to human standards, all our actions may be complete failures. The Cross was the greatest failure ever beheld on earth, and yet the greatest and the most complete triumph.

O sorely tried and sorrowing soul, thou who art grieving disconsolately over love fruitlessly spent on a work very dear to thee, it is the very disappointment that will purify and spiritualize thy love and so bind thee more closely to Christ, for spiritual development is the effect of relinquishing what nature prizes most and clings to most tenaciously.

We must try to realize (and how comforting it will be!) that the suffering Savior now dwells in Heaven with the same human heart that on earth felt the weight of every sorrow and pain which we feel, one with us in sympathy with every form of trial that besets mortals during life's warfare, and, consequently, tenderly sensitive to all our needs in the struggle whose issue is eternal. That heart, most gentle and acutely touched at the sight of our sufferings, now throbs by the side of the eternal Father. The God-Man who drained the cup of sorrow now lovingly pleads, as He did on earth, with us who labor and are heavily burdened, to come to Him, and He will give us rest.[126]

What solace in the thought that there is a common bond of sympathy through community of trial between us and Christ! What peace of mind despite our weakness, our ingratitude, our

[126] Cf. Matt. 11:28-29.

sin! What fears nonetheless instinctively seize us as we contemplate the possibility of our hearts' not beating in unison with His or our placing an obstacle to our union with Him by our failure to appreciate the chastening influence of self-sacrifice — in a word, by our want of charity.

In order that our lives might be the same as His, the God of love gave us the commandment that would be a perpetual reminder of Him and the badge of His disciples. "This is my commandment," says Christ, "that you love one another, as I have loved you."[127] "By this shall all men know that you are my disciples: if you have love one for another."[128] This commandment identifies us with the deepest source of life in God, which is love. "Let us love one another, for charity is of God. Everyone that loveth is born of God and knoweth God. . . . If we love one another, God abideth in us, and His charity is perfected in us. . . . God is charity: and he that abideth in charity, abideth in God, and God in him."[129]

[127] John 15:12.
[128] John 13:35.
[129] 1 John 4:7, 12, 16.

Chapter Five

Recognize the
depths of Christ's love
in His Passion

∞

During the first part of the Passion, which closed with the agony, Christ suffered only mentally. In the second part, which ended with His death, the Redeemer was tortured in both soul and body, draining the chalice to the dregs. The two constituted "the baptism wherewith I am to be baptized"[130] — the baptism symbolizing the external suffering inflicted on Him by His enemies, and the chalice which He had to drink indicating the mental anguish which He acutely experienced in the secret recess of His soul. At this stage of the Passion, we must realize fully that Christ was God as well as man, and emphasize the fact that He signed His condemnation to death by openly professing His divinity. His solemn declaration that He was God made the Jews exclaim, when Pilate offered to release Him, "Not this man, but Barabbas."[131] The rise of the sinner against Him who, being in the form of man, asserted and proved that He was God, the rejection of God by fallen humanity, consummated Christ's crucifixion.

The raising of Lazarus inspired the determination to put Christ to death. This stupendous miracle demonstrated the Savior's divinity and filled the multitude that witnessed it

[130] Luke 12:50.
[131] John 18:40.

with enthusiasm so overwhelming that it only intensified the uncompromising hatred of the chief priests and ancients of the people, who "from that day . . . devised to put Him to death."[132]

∞

Christ was rejected as God and as man

In all the judicial processes through which Christ passed, His claim to divinity elicited the last word from His judges. Three times the Savior faced trial. After His capture, He was led into the house of Caiphas. False witnesses were suborned, but Jesus was silent. His absolute silence enraged the high priest and extorted from him the charge of blasphemy: "I adjure Thee, by the living God," said Caiphas, in the form of a challenge which an Israelite had to answer, "that Thou tell us if Thou be the Christ, the Son of God." "Jesus saith to him, 'Thou hast said it. Nevertheless I say to you, hereafter you shall see the Son of Man sitting on the right hand of the power of God and coming in the clouds of Heaven.' Then the high priest rent his garments, saying, 'He hath blasphemed; what further need have we of witnesses? Behold, now you have heard the blasphemy. What think you?' But they answering, said, 'He is guilty of death.' "[133]

As soon as it was day, the Redeemer was brought before the council, or Sanhedrin. The judges vainly strove to disguise their hatred for Christ by trying to brand Him with some vague charge. A second time He was accosted: "If Thou be the

[132] John 11:53.
[133] Matt. 26:63-66.

Christ, tell us."[134] But the question was put ambiguously, for "the Christ" might have meant to the Jew only an earthly Messiah. And Christ replied, "If I shall tell you, you will not believe me. And if I shall also ask you, you will not answer me, nor let me go. But hereafter the Son of Man shall be sitting on the right hand of the power of God."[135] But the third time, there is not even the suspicion of doubt about the inquiry, for the question is couched in the clearest possible language: "Art Thou, then, the Son of God?" And Christ answered, "You say that I am." And they said, "What need we any further testimony? For we ourselves have heard it from His own mouth."[136]

Christ was finally led to Pilate, and, after the Jews had fruitlessly endeavored to convict the Savior on a civil charge, for the third and last time the same eternally significant question was put to Him, and it forced from the vacillating Roman governor Christ's condemnation. "We have a law," they shouted, "and according to the law, He ought to die, because He made Himself the Son of God."[137] The assertion that He was God signed the Savior's death warrant. "He came unto His own, and His own received him not";[138] both Jew and Gentile rejected Christ because He claimed to be God.

Never was there such a rejection, stimulated as it was by the rage and the malice of Hell; a rejection that flung wide open

[134] Luke 22:66.
[135] Luke 22:67-69.
[136] Luke 22:70-71.
[137] John 19:7.
[138] John 1:11.

the floodgates of human wickedness, the tempest swelling to immeasurable heights; a rejection that made Christ's last night on earth the darkest and the most revolting that ever followed day. Unable to brook Christ's presence in His own world, sinful humanity, aided and abetted by the infernal powers, sought most brutally to drive Him out of it.

But sin attacking God sounded its own death knell, because the Redeemer, in enduring the punishment incident to sin, was condemning it and, at the infinite price of His blood, was delivering the sinner from its eternal curse.

Christ's rejection as God was, however, only a part of His suffering and humiliation. Pilate's words: "Behold the Man,"[139] a last powerful appeal to the sinner's sense of compassion, fell on deaf ears. Even the Savior's outraged sinless humanity was utterly despised by the sinner when he exclaimed, "Not this man, but Barabbas," as if he yearned for sin to triumph completely over Christ both as God and man.

The depths of degradation were reached when Pilate's question: "What will you, then, that I do to the king of the Jews?" was answered by the most diabolical cry ever shrieked by man in his wildest frenzy: "Crucify Him."[140] In the original Greek, it is not "Crucify Him," but simply "Crucify." Christ's person is not mentioned; His humanity is condemned; His existence is loathed, is not even recognized. Thus did He literally become what had been prophesied of Him: "a worm, and no man."[141]

[139] John 19:5.
[140] Mark 15:12-13.
[141] Ps. 21:7 (RSV = Ps. 22:6).

74

∞

Christ suffered all the punishment for man's sins

But this was not enough. Christ had to descend to the abyss of sorrow and shame before the souls of sinners were redeemed. The closing hours of the Passion prove this. The crisis of the Savior's sufferings — who can describe it? Words cannot depict the agonizing Redeemer, the baptism of blood eternally decreed by the Triune God, which Christ had envisaged all during the eternal years, long before the dawn of creation and upon which, throughout the ages, the Holy Spirit had shed His prophetic light. This baptism was prefigured for centuries by innumerable sacrifices of blood and heralded by the daily ministrations of diverse orders of priesthood, so that this overwhelming mystery might seize man's deepest consciousness. Christ had unceasingly preached it by word and act, so that His elect might enliven their faith in this prodigy of infinite charity, which, by prayer and loneliness and pain, by hidden, consuming grief of soul, He had for thirty-three years prepared Himself to undergo as the crowning act of a life of absolute self-oblation. What unspeakable wonder veils, what mysterious preparation precedes, this most profoundly significant event in the history of the world!

The yearning to die, manifested by full surrender to the will of the eternal Father during the agony, now issues in action. The distinct feature of this last scene of the Passion is this: Christ now experiences the almost insupportable burden of the punishment inflicted upon Him for the sins of humanity and the burden of death, their eternal curse. Stooping down and meeting humanity on its lowest level, the Godhead is now laden with the sins of the world for all time and, in assuming them, bears also their awful chastisement. The load of iniquity oppresses Christ as if He were the guilty culprit. The personal union of the divine and human natures gave to the blood of the Redeemer its infinite value, its power of full satisfaction to the eternal Father, thus making the sufferings of the Savior the sufferings of God.

The death-agony of Christ may be divided into two distinct periods. During the first period, the brilliant eastern sun shines brightly upon the face of the Redeemer, streaming with blood, and upon the multitude standing around the Cross. The crowd, with curses and blasphemies on their lips, with the triumphant glare of Hell darting from their eyes, now press to and fro, now stand staring. Their ribald jests and hateful malice taint the air. Throughout this period, although the agony of death has seized Him, Christ gazes upon the multitude with eternal pity, lavishing upon their souls the love that His Church would, under the guidance of the Holy Spirit, perpetuate through the ages. The prayer for His crucifiers, the absolution of the penitent thief, the bestowal of His own Mother to be their mother[142] — these three utterances bring to a close the first period.

∽

Christ suffered the darkness of God's abandonment

After the Savior had revealed the love for man, sealed in His blood, by giving the Virgin Mother as His dying legacy to the world, He prepared, silent and solitary, to undergo the final suffering of His Passion. The last act of the drama prolific of

[142] Luke 23:33, 42; John 19:26.

eternal happiness for sinners now begins, the climax of its extreme pain. The darkness which, the evangelist states, covered the earth from the sixth to the ninth hour,[143] typified the interior gloom darkening the agonizing soul of Jesus Christ. Into this black solitude of ghastly horror, the Redeemer enters to complete His act of infinite love.

The noise around the Cross now yields to profound silence. The coarse talk, the curses and blasphemies, are heard no more. The sin and confusion of the Holy City are swallowed up in the appalling darkness. Beneath the Cross, all is still. The one sound, which emphasizes the solemn silence, is the constant dripping of the precious blood.

Thoughts doubtless hurried through the mind of the inhumanly taunted and outraged Savior as death violently attacked Him: the thought of His loving acceptance of the enormous burden of man's sins as His own; the consciousness of the sins of the past; the knowledge of the sins of the future and the realization of their injury to men; the consciousness of the powers of Hell terrorizing His soul, weak beyond words and sinking fast in the last agony of death. All this mental pain was an essential part of the sacrifice that saved the sinner.

About the ninth hour, Christ reached the crisis of His sorrow and suffering: His abandonment by His Father. During His sojourn on earth, the Redeemer was "the reproach of men and the outcast of the people,"[144] but He ever communed with Him whose will was the meat by which He lived.[145] Now He

[143] Matt. 27:45; Mark 15:33; Luke 23:43.
[144] Ps. 21:7 (RSV = Ps. 22:6).
[145] Cf. John 4:34.

passes through the gulf created by sin between man and God. That the sinner might be forever associated with Him, He unites Himself to the sinner, feeling with divine keenness the separation from God and the spiritual desolation wrought by sin in the sinner's soul. In His solitary loneliness, He loudly cries out, not as in the garden, "My Father," but as wholly forsaken humanity deprived of the support and comfort of the Godhead. His soul, enshrouded with the spiritual gloom of falling nature, pleads beseechingly with the Father, and the woeful cry, "My God, my God, why hast Thou forsaken me?"[146] mounts to Heaven.

It was love rising to the height of perfect self-abandonment, and reconciling the lost world with the Father by its docile obedience unto the death of the Cross, which was required by the God of infinite sanctity from Him who had assumed flesh to satisfy effectually for the sins of men.

But sorrow speaks no more in pain. Pain has spent itself in that last pitiful cry. Beneath the Cross, a change is visible. The darkness has affrighted the multitude. The silence is broken by the noisy activity of the soldiers and by the remark doubtfully expressed: "This man calleth Elijah."[147]

∞

Christ's perfect self-abandonment
brought Him peace

But Christ's sufferings have ceased. Now, probably, light begins to dispel the darkness. In the sorrowful heart of Christ,

---

[146] Matt. 27:46; Mark 15:34.
[147] Cf. Matt. 27:47.

the depressed powers and emotions revive. A serene peace hovers over the stricken soul before it departs. The voice assumes a different tone in uttering the last words. Restful assurance and a calm repose are evident in its accents, exclaiming, "I thirst."[148] Triumphant rejoicing after long and weary labor and exulting anticipation of eternal rest vitalize His words: "It is consummated."[149]

Christ's agony is over. Like one delivered from a terrible struggle to enjoy the spoils of victory, Christ breathes His last word: "Father, into Thy hands I commend my spirit."[150] He bows His head, not because of weak human nature, but of His own will, giving back to the Father His soul to be glorified forever with the redeemed souls of men.

It was the climax of lifelong obedience. Willingly had He accepted the profound humiliations of His Passion; willingly did He give His life. But, having satisfied divine justice by dying, He took up His life again, so that His death might not be a "stumbling block, and . . . foolishness" to those who believe, but the "power of God and the wisdom of God."[151]

∽

Contemplating the Passion should
fill you with gratitude and contrition

The contemplation of this blessed mystery is so absorbing that it rids us of any thought of self, banishes all self-interest.

[148] John 19:28.
[149] John 19:30.
[150] Luke 23:46.
[151] 1 Cor. 1:23-24.

We cannot, however, meditate on Christ's death without reflecting on its deep meaning for ourselves.

What joy thrills the heart and soul fully conscious that sin has been blotted out and the sinner reconciled with the eternal Father, through the death of His divine Son, Christ our Redeemer! But the keenest joy flows, not from the knowledge that our sins have been forgiven, but from the consideration of the means by which they were forgiven. Eternal death wrought by sin met Christ, eternal life, in a mighty struggle and was conquered forever in the most marvelous mystery of love ever enacted on earth.

Reflection on the death of Christ begets contrition. The realization of the malice of sin — the spiritual ruin that it works in souls, the Son of God shedding tears over it, the evils that it has introduced into the world, the everlasting punishment awaiting it — will inspire imperfect contrition. But the apprehension of this saving mystery should penetrate into the depths of our souls and awaken perfect contrition. We must possess the living consciousness that sin crushed the heart of Christ and made Him tread the winepress of sorrow and suffering beyond description, and that neither the holocausts nor the penances of centuries, but only the blood of the infinite God, could wipe out even one sin. These should generate perfect contrition by kindling in our hearts that pure love of God for His own sake that will, with touching tenderness, bind us to Him forever.

Greatness stricken with sorrow, majesty bowed down to the dust — is there any thought more awe-inspiring? Here is the eternal God dying for His guilty creatures: a God weeping, a God scourged, a God crowned with thorns, a God spit upon, a God crucified! And we have clearly been the cause of it all! What will become of us if we reject this astounding revelation of divine love? Like Jerusalem, which rejected Christ and steeled itself against the insistent, eternal pleadings of His love, we, too, shall be left desolate.

Christ yearned to die for us. Who, then, can understand the bitterness of His disappointment when He finds no response in our lives to the lessons that He teaches with divine eloquence from the Cross? The greater the sacrifice involved in a work, the keener the disappointment when the work fails. Ideals long cherished, ardently loved, but never realized blight the soul with a sorrow unspeakable. This is the grief that seizes the heart of Christ when we, by sin, trample upon His precious blood!

∞

Your own self-denial must be conformed to Christ's

The crucified Savior teaches us one comprehensive lesson that embraces the patience, humility, and strength of will which were the very life of this mystery. It is the lesson of self-denial. This we must learn before we can learn any other lesson. To forego self is more heroic than to forego the world, for the world is what self makes it. But the world may be overcome and the self be still triumphant.

To learn the lesson from the Cross is to suppress some feature of complex self-indulgence. Some elements of self either have never naturally revealed themselves or have been stifled by environment. Because we generally assume the tone of the circle in which we move, education and social interchanges are powerful factors in eliminating a particular form of self-assertion. Our life's work is another remarkable influence in extinguishing, or at least neutralizing, other elements of self. Incalculable evil has been controlled, even temporarily conquered, by some such counteracting antidote not of our own making. But this feature of self-denial does not conform us to Christ.

Our besetting passion, our marked moral weakness, our special sinful tendency — this is the self that must be overcome. Does this stand immovable in the presence of the Cross? Can anger that quickly begets rage, or love of money that swiftly becomes avarice, or pride that brooks no restraint, or sensitiveness that forever creates imaginary injuries, or love of ease that tolerates no exertion of mind or body, or vanity that loves praise bear the touch of the Cross? Does any moral weakness whatever dominate our spiritual lives in the shadow of the Cross? If it does, we are not conformed to Christ, and Him crucified.

Perhaps we carry the Cross, but without resignation to the divine will. We may, in this state, long to submit ourselves to the suffering Savior who seeks to impress His image indelibly upon us. But this is not to know Christ and "the fellowship of His sufferings."[152] Perhaps we bear the Cross with a proneness to murmur. We are not Christ's yet, but are being drawn to Him. To accept the Cross under the wondrous efficacy of grace, gratefully and with absolute submission; to restrain every natural craving contrary to the divine law, to crucify the flesh — this is the indisputable proof that we are dead with Christ, and

[152] Phil. 3:10.

it will enable us to rise glorious and immortal with Him. For "Christ died for all, that they also who live may not now live to themselves, but unto Him who died for them, and rose again."[153]

[153] 2 Cor. 5:15.

Chapter Six

∾

Surrender yourself
to God's will

∞

By Original Sin, man forfeited his title to eternal bliss and consigned the human race to unending misery. But although outraged by His disobedient creature, the infinitely merciful Creator lovingly resolved "to seek and to save that which was lost."[154] To do this, He chose from the children of men a Being who would reconcile man with his offended God by willingly bearing in His own person the burden of man's sin. This chosen Mediator was thus to satisfy the justice of God, give Him greater glory than that of which man had robbed Him by sin, and exalt man to a dignity sublimer than that which he had lost by his disloyalty.

Unlike the rest of mortals, this Mediator had to be not only sinless, but unutterably holy. Only then could He offer to God a sacrifice commensurate with His infinite sanctity. But no creature, however holy, could fully atone for sin. As the value of an act is measured by the dignity of the person performing it, such satisfaction, finite in itself, assumed infinite value by reason of Him who satisfied, and, being infinite in value, it could not be rejected by the sovereign majesty of the Godhead. Hence, only God incarnate could be the Mediator between earth and Heaven. He had to be made flesh to endure

[154]Luke 19:10.

the chastisement due to sin. He had to be God to pay fully man's debt to divine justice and to be a sacrificial victim worthy of the holiness of the eternal Father.

What a marvelous prodigy of divine ingenuity is the mystery of the Incarnation, the fathomless depths of which should reveal the atrocity of sin, both with regard to God and to ourselves! So great is the malice of sin that the combined sufferings of the human race for all eternity could not atone for it. Only God made man could expiate it, and, in His love for the sinner, He underwent a Passion and death whose bitterness and humiliation are indescribable. To satisfy for sin, Christ became an outcast for sinners, bearing their curse as if it fell on Him and not on them, feeling in His deepest soul the desolate loneliness of their abandoned state — a holocaust for them to appease the justice of an angry God.

∞

Christ's death was an act of Redemption

Holy Scripture is eloquently simple, but withal most comprehensive, in portraying the barbarous treatment, the repulsive horrors, of which the merciful Savior was the innocent victim. "Christ," explains St. Paul to the Galatians, "hath redeemed us from the curse of the law, being made a curse for us: for it is written: Cursed is everyone that hangeth on a tree."[155] And to the Corinthians he writes, "Him who knew no sin, He hath made sin for us, that we might be made the justice of God in Him."[156] Isaiah draws a powerful picture of

[155] Gal. 3:13.
[156] 2 Cor. 5:21.

Christ's heart-rending plight. "Who is this," exclaims the prophet, "that cometh from Edom, with dyed garments from Bosra, this beautiful one in his robe, walking in the greatness of his strength? . . . Why, then, is thy apparel red, and thy garments like theirs that tread in the winepress? 'I have trodden the winepress alone, and of the Gentiles, there is not a man with me.' "[157] "Surely he hath borne our infirmities and carried our sorrows, and we have thought him, as it were, a leper, and as one struck by God and afflicted. But he was wounded for our iniquities, he was bruised for our sins; the chastisement of our peace was upon him, and by his bruises we are healed. All we like sheep have gone astray; every one hath turned aside into his own way; and the Lord hath laid on him the iniquity of us all. He was offered because it was his own will, and he opened not his mouth; he shall be led as a sheep to the slaughter, and shall be dumb as a lamb before his shearer, and he shall not open his mouth. He was taken away from distress, and from judgment: who shall declare his generation? Because he is cut off out of the land of the living: for the wickedness of my people have I struck him."[158]

This very expressive language of Sacred Scripture proves that the death of Christ was essentially more than an act of heroic self-oblation for the truth, a mere giving of Himself to the cruel torments of His Passion in order to raise man to the sublime heights of moral exaltation. The infinite Lover of souls, by His death, wiped out "the handwriting of the decree that was against us, which was contrary to us. And He hath

[157] Isa. 63:1-3.
[158] Isa. 53:4-8.

taken the same out of the way, fastening it to the Cross,"[159] satisfying the justice of God and reuniting us with Him through the infinite power of the blood which He shed so freely for us. If Christ did not satisfy for our sins, what meaning, then, have the words of St. John: "He is the propitiation for our sins"?[160] St. Paul's words also become unintelligible, for it was only by being made a curse for us that Christ redeemed us from the curse of the law. Again, why did the Father, to use the words of the great apostle, make the divine Son to be sin for us,[161] if not to expiate our sin? Sin, in this instance, means not only the evil itself, but also the atonement for it.

But, although Christ assumed the burden of man's sin and united Himself most intimately with man's fallen nature, the consciousness of sin in itself was not His, but only its punishment. Christ was the innocent Lamb of God, His humanity being sinless in virtue of its personal union with the Godhead. To suppose the contrary would be to nullify the effect of His Passion and death, which derive their value solely from the infinite preciousness of His blood.

Nor did Christ's assumption of the burden of man's sin make Him, as if He were the guilty culprit and not the sinless victim, the object of the Father's almighty wrath. How could the Father be angry with Him with whom He was eternally one? How could He vent His infinite vengeance on Him, when the mutual love of the Father and Son was coeval with Their very existence?

[159] Col. 2:14.
[160] 1 John 2:2.
[161] Cf. 2 Cor. 5:21.

The agony is a very practical example of this truth. At the climax of His wrestling with death, when His human soul sank beneath the load of the world's sin, Christ was fully conscious of the indissoluble tie that bound Him to the Father. In Gethsemane, as throughout the rest of the Passion, there was complete identity of thought and desire between the Father and the Son. Christ in the garden wholly realized the bond of the eternal sonship. Even in His abandonment, when it seemed that He had lost entirely all consciousness of the Godhead, even in this crisis of loneliest desolation, He cried out, "My God!" Never for an instant, in that period of profoundest oppression, when Christ's heavily laden soul descended into the abyss of overwhelming woe, was there any suspension of the sense of divine Sonship.

Besides, what would be the significance of the Sacrifice of the Mass in commemorating and perpetuating the work of our Redemption if it represented on the part of Christ only an act, not of expiation, but of wondrous heroism? If Christ did not shed His blood unto the remission of sins, there would be no need of a priesthood and no Mass as a sacrifice of propitiation.

∾

Christ calls you to die to yourself

But the mere death of Christ did not reconcile man with his God. It was the absolute surrender of Himself by perfect obedience to the will of His Father that made His oblation on Calvary eternally efficacious for sinners. How truly obedient was Christ! He sealed His obedience with His death.

The depths of Christ's abasement must ever be the measure of our spiritual sublimation. He assumed our nature, lavishing upon us His divinity. He came that we might "have life and . . . have it more abundantly."[162] Inestimably great, magnificently grand is the Christian's destiny. If he is to attain it, he must "put . . . on the Lord Jesus Christ."[163] To live for Christ alone, and to die to all else — such should be the conduct of him whose soul has been consecrated to God by Baptism. The Christian must try to scale the lofty heights of the supernatural life of Christ, striving might and main to die to himself, so that he may be united heart and soul with his God. Then will he be able to say with St. Paul, "I live, now not I, but Christ liveth in me. And that I live now in the flesh, I live in the faith of the Son of God, who loved me, and delivered Himself for me."[164] Then will he, through the manifold energies of grace, daily grow more and more like Christ, because his will is one with the divine will.

The victory of the supernatural over the natural, the triumph of sanctity within us, cannot but follow moral death to self. We must die to ourselves so that we may imitate Christ's life of transcendent love, for sacrifice is the touchstone of love, the infallible measure of its strength, its very law. Christ pleased not Himself. "I came down from Heaven," He exclaimed, "not to do my own will, but the will of Him that sent me."[165] He dedicated every thought, every word, every act to the salvation of souls. Constant self-oblation for souls was the essence of His life. He lived and died for sinners.

[162] John 10:10.
[163] Rom. 13:14.
[164] Gal. 2:20.
[165] John 6:38.

The highest ideal possible to human nature is a life of perennial self-denial for others, because it was the life eternally decreed by the Father for His divine Son. And what suffering Christ underwent, what sorrow He experienced, living such a life!

Even now, although He does not live this life in hardships, humiliations, and shame, He continues to lead it "always living to make intercession for us."[166] Whatever the outward form of this life may be, inwardly it is always the same. The external circumstances — the time, the place, the manner — of Christ's life of sacrifice were sunk in His total commendation of Himself to the will of His Father. This is not to say that He was immune to the least intimation of pain or failed to feel with divine keenness the anguish of His sacrifice for sinners, but the accomplishment of His Father's will was so dear to Him that He was utterly indifferent to the visible shape which any phase of His self-oblation might assume. Such was the life of Christ, the tenor of which minutely revealed the love of His eternal Father for Him.

Our lives must be the same if we are to be conformed to "Jesus Christ and Him crucified."[167] Whatever form of suffering afflicts us, however heavy our cross, we must accept it with unflinching courage, so that, in our following Christ, His image may be indelibly impressed upon our souls.

Very often, little or no success may attend our best efforts. Was there ever a greater failure, humanly speaking, than the Cross? Perhaps our burden is made heavier because we feel

[166] Heb. 7:25.
[167] 1 Cor. 2:2.

that we bear it alone. Christ looked "for one that would comfort Him and found none."[168] We may be the victims of the unreasonableness of our neighbor. Christ was "a worm, and no man"[169] in the hands of sinners. Perhaps the crudest ingratitude requites our ministrations of loving kindness. Christ was denied by Peter and betrayed by Judas — His apostles, to whom He had said, "I will not now call you servants, for the servant knoweth not what his lord doth. But I have called you friends, because all things whatsoever I have heard of my Father, I have made known to you."[170] Are our motives impugned? Maliciously false witnesses sentenced the Redeemer to death. Are the lives of others thrilled with heartening joy, and ours replete with withering sorrow? Christ, "having joy set before Him, endured the Cross, despising the shame."[171] Do we suffer without comfort, bereft of all sympathy, sorrow blighting our daily lives? On the Cross, Christ deprived Himself of the consolation of the Godhead, the Father veiling His face in the crisis of the Savior's Crucifixion.

∞

Your sufferings will bring you a reward

Conformity to the crucified Christ must be the supreme passion of our souls. We must detach ourselves decisively and irrevocably from all that is earthly and by faith rise up to the God who alone can satisfy this passion. "The whole life of

[168] Cf. Ps. 68:21 (RSV = Ps. 69:20).
[169] Ps. 21:7 (RSV = Ps. 22:6).
[170] John 15:15.
[171] Heb. 12:2.

Christ was a cross and a martyrdom."[172] He had, like us, a human heart, and His glorious human soul was affrighted by suffering. But one thought sustained Him throughout His Passion and in the anguish of His death: their eternal results. We, too, must be absorbed by the habitual contemplation of our wondrous end, ever bearing in mind the eternal reward of temporal suffering, for our end is the same as Christ's. The means of realizing our exalted destiny, the shape and form of suffering, should not concern us. A life of pain is ours; the form of its manifestation in us, its minute details, are for God to determine.

Then, too, we cannot always foresee our trials and thus brace our spiritual energy to meet them. At times, they attack us suddenly, when, perhaps, we are least prepared to encounter them. Absolute submission to God, casting all our care upon Him until He either mercifully removes the cross or tempers the bitterness of pain by giving us the light requisite to see its eternal import in the divine plan of salvation, is what we urgently need, because we are free to choose between good and evil, not between joy and sorrow.

To resist the unbalanced demands of nature, to be true lovers of the crucified Savior, to conquer self, by becoming daily, through the purifying power of suffering, more like Christ — such must be our fixed resolve, if we are to "walk worthy of the vocation in which we are called."[173]

Whatever our lot in life, however limited our sphere of action, in order to follow Christ, we must deny ourselves. In the

[172] *Imitation of Christ*, Bk. 2, ch. 12.
[173] Eph. 4:1.

struggle for salvation we should stimulate our ambition by the strength and the impetus of impulse that thrills the heart, the eternal recompense of self-sacrifice. We must rise far above externals. Not the Cross in any particular form, but the result of carrying it or of being nailed to it, must be the idea that engrosses us.

Dominated by this idea, we will not shrink from preference given to another, to our utter humiliation, from the most acute interior anguish, or from the abyss of exterior suffering. Nor will we yield to natural inconstancy and, as the wail of our sore distress mounts upward to God, ask Him to change a jot or tittle of the outward feature of our crucifixion in the realization of our special calling. In full possession of our souls through patience, we will commend ourselves to the crucified Christ until we can exclaim with Him, "It is consummated."[174]

Confidence in God will then be the anchor of our earthly exile, sweetening, through conformity to the divine will, the bitterness of our sorrow and lightening our cross. The Lord is "my firmament and my refuge."[175] "The Lord is my strength . . . my helper and my redeemer."[176] "In my affliction, I called upon the Lord, and I cried to my God, and He heard my voice from His holy Temple, and my cry before Him came into His ears."[177]

The consciousness of eternal joy following temporal trial will hearten us. "The sufferings of this time are not worthy to

[174] John 19:30.
[175] Ps.70:3 (RSV = Ps. 71:3).
[176] Ps. 117:14, 18:15 (RSV = Ps. 118:14, 19:14).
[177] Ps. 17:7 (RSV = 18:6).

be compared with the glory to come, that shall be revealed in us."[178] How utterly insignificant will the pressure of present pain, the work done for God, the humiliations borne for Him who "emptied Himself"[179] for us sinners and the love purified and deepened by life's disappointments and heartaches all appear when we shall have entered "the house of our eternity,"[180] where our "sorrow shall be turned into joy"[181] — where "neither shall the sun fall on them, nor any heat. For the Lamb, which is in the midst of the throne, shall rule them . . . who are come out of great tribulation . . . and shall lead them to the fountains of the waters of life, and God shall wipe away all tears from their eyes."[182] There we "shall be inebriated with the plenty" of God's house and "delight in the Lord" forever.[183]

[178] Rom. 8:18.
[179] Phil. 2:7.
[180] Cf. Eccles. 12:5.
[181] John 16:20.
[182] Cf. Apoc. 7:14, 16-17 (RSV = Rev. 7:14, 16-17).
[183] Cf. Ps. 35:9, 36:4 (RSV = Ps. 36:8, 37:4).

John A. Kane
(1883-1962)

∞

Born in Philadelphia in 1883, John Kane attended St. Mary's Seminary in Baltimore, Maryland, and St. Charles Borromeo Seminary in Overbrook, Pennsylvania, and was ordained for the Archdiocese of Philadelphia in 1912.

Known for his devotion to the Holy Eucharist, Fr. Kane was the first pastor in his archdiocese to introduce and to receive permission to hold all-night adoration of the Blessed Sacrament. He placed great importance on Catholic education of the young and succeeded in filling to overflowing his parish school of St. Madeline's in Ridley Park. In addition, he actively sought to educate adults in their Faith, and he was a pioneer in initiating a weekly religion class for them.

Fr. Kane was known during his lifetime for his great love of prayer and meditation, and his several books give proof of the wisdom gleaned from so many hours of contemplation. His writings bespeak a profound love of Christ and a warm understanding of the Catholic layman's struggle to achieve holiness. His words offer Catholics practical insight and encouragement to seek a deeper union and friendship with God.

∞

Sophia Institute Press®

∞

Sophia Institute is a nonprofit institution that seeks to restore man's knowledge of eternal truth, including man's knowledge of his own nature, his relation to other persons, and his relation to God. Sophia Institute Press® serves this end in numerous ways: it publishes translations of foreign works to make them accessible to English-speaking readers; it brings out-of-print books back into print; and it publishes important new books that fulfill the ideals of Sophia Institute. These books afford readers a rich source of the enduring wisdom of mankind.

Sophia Institute Press® makes these high-quality books available to the general public by using advanced technology and by soliciting donations to subsidize its general publishing costs. Your generosity can help Sophia Institute Press® to provide the public with editions of works containing the enduring wisdom of the ages. Please send your tax-deductible contribution to the address below. We also welcome your questions, comments, and suggestions.

For your free catalog, call:
Toll-free: 1-800-888-9344

or write:
Sophia Institute Press®
Box 5284, Manchester, NH 03108

or visit our website:
www.sophiainstitute.com

Sophia Institute is a tax-exempt institution as defined by the Internal Revenue Code, Section 501(c)(3). Tax I.D. 22-2548708.